Advance Praise for *The Gospel a*

"If you're Christian, American, and intelligent and if you have time to read only one book about how to be all three of those things simultaneously, choose this one. I don't agree with everything David Dark says, but in *The Gospel according to America*, his already established penchant for edgy observation has matured into something frighteningly close to wisdom."

—Phyllis Tickle, author, lecturer, and commentator

"David Dark is a schoolteacher. In *The Gospel according to America*, he takes us into his classroom, and it is so reminiscent of Athens that we realize why the hemlock was prescribed."

—Will Campbell, preacher, farmer, social activist, and author of *Soul Among Lions* and *Brother to a Dragonfly*

"If I prayed, I would pray for all the David Darks—all the smart, funny, thoughtful, quirky, tough-minded, well-read, culturally engaged Christians in America—to arise and speak up. I know that the crabbed, mean, unthinking forms and flavors of political Christianity that I see portrayed every day in the media are not the whole story."

—Kurt Andersen, author of *Turn of the Century* and host of public radio's *Studio 360*

"In days when disturbingly large sectors of America seem to have slipped into a holy warrior trance, when the borders between American self-interest and the kingdom of God are fuzzier than ever in the minds of churchgoers and politicians alike, David Dark's book comes like a bucket of cold water to the face. Is this a young Wendell Berry among us—combining intelligent faith with social conscience and cultural awareness? His incisive yet subtle style may make you think so. I underlined paragraph after paragraph and am a new fan of this brilliant young writer."

—Brian D. McLaren, pastor and author of *A Generous Orthodoxy* and *A New Kind of Christian*

THE GOSPEL
ACCORDING TO AMERICA

A MEDITATION ON A GOD-BLESSED, CHRIST-HAUNTED IDEA

David Dark

WESTMINSTER
JOHN KNOX PRESS
LOUISVILLE · KENTUCKY

Book design by Sharon Adams
Cover design by Jennifer K. Cox
Cover art: God Bless America Flag @ Joseph Sohm; Visions of America/ CORBIS

First edition
Published by Westminster John Knox Press
Louisville, Kentucky

This book is printed on acid-free paper that meets the American National Standards Institute Z39.48 standard. ∞

PRINTED IN THE UNITED STATES OF AMERICA

05 06 07 08 09 10 11 12 13 14 — 10 9 8 7 6 5 4 3 2 1

Library of Congress Cataloging-in-Publication Data

Dark, David
  The gospel according to America : a meditation on a God-blessed, Christ-haunted idea / David Dark.— 1st ed.
    p. cm.
  Includes bibliographical references.
  ISBN 0-664-22769-4 (alk. paper)
    1. United States—Church history. 2. Church and state—United States. 3. Christianity and culture—United States. I. Title.

  BR526.D36 2004
  277.3'083—dc22

                                        2004056126

To my father, Joel Dark Sr., who kept me amused over all the ways
a righteous God will offend our sense of righteousness.

And to my mother, Doris Dark, who keeps me awake to all the
strange new ways I have yet to love the people
with whom I disagree.

Contents

Acknowledgments

I owe constant gratitude to my wife, Sarah, who suggested this book and whose passionate, determined, and long-term affection for neighbors and any presumed enemies keeps me thinking straight. I'm also indebted to the Masens, the Darks, the Wileys, and the Foremans for their consistent support and their patience when I get to rambling on like a demon-possessed man. For exemplifying the kind of conversations that make disagreement a breakthrough rather than an awkward ending, I must thank Todd Greene, Phil Boeing, Geoff Little, Ed Kelly, Douglas Sharp, Lee Smithey, Tom Wills, Gar Saeger, Steve Stockman, Frank Masen, Trevor Henderson, Rob Bancroft, Richard Goode, Rodney Clapp, Dwight Ozard, John Wilson, Douglas Kaine McKelvey, and Ken Locke. I have also come to depend on certain voices in recent history, and without their example and their careful articulation of a theopolitical imagination, the present work would not have been possible. As a cloud of witnesses to a culture of life with which this work aspires to be in some degree of continuity, the following figures don't appear in these pages, but my debts should be evident to anyone who knows their work: Marva Dawn, John Paul II, Czeslaw Milosz, Rich Mullins, Robert McAfee Brown, Walter Brueggemann, and Eugene Peterson. Special thanks are due to David Dobson and Julie Tonini for their patience and attentiveness to the manuscript.

Instead of an Introduction:
Remembrance Belongs to the People

*L*ike many Americans, my father was haunted by the Bible. Figuring out what it said, what it all meant, and how to live a life somehow faithful to it was a lifelong obsession. The Bible was always in the back of his mind. Like a leather-bound black hole, it pulled on his thoughts, painted the matter-of-fact a different color, called into question whatever anybody nearby described as common sense, and uproariously unsettled the agreed-upon obvious of every scenario. It was the measure of authenticity for all speech, and speech that presumed to have its backing ("It's biblical," "According to the Bible," "God says . . .") was to be viewed with particular scrutiny and suspicion, because the Bible belonged to everyone and no one. It was nobody's property. Always dangerous, a double-edged sword. Like absolute truth, it's out there, but anyone who presumed to own its copyright was criminally insane.

With this vibe at work throughout my growing-up years, my father made it very difficult for anyone in our family to keep religion and politics in their assigned categories, because the Bible, as he read it, didn't go for that kind of thing. He understood as well as anyone that there is a hard-won arrangement at work in America whereby we're expected to keep our talk of the Lord, eternal salvation, and a certain coming kingdom out of "the business world," "politics," and whatever the polity seems to agree on as "polite conversation." But the demands of genuinely candid exchange, with all the hilarity and illumination that frank discussion can promise, would not allow such deluded misconceptions about what any of us are *really* talking about.

He spent too much time exchanging jokes and anecdotes at our nearby Waffle House and holding forth in conversation with Muslim gas station attendants for the public/private distinctions in political and religious matters to ever really hold absolute sway. And in the deepest sense, he didn't think it polite or even friendly to pretend that certain elephants aren't in the room; that Jesus of Nazareth has very little to say about a nation's talk of wars on terror or that the demands of Allah or Jehovah upon humankind can be conveniently sequestered within the "spirituality" section of the global market. Without a costly commitment to candor among family and potential friends, the possibility of truthful conversation (a prerequisite for the formation of more perfect unions) begins to tragically diminish, and responsible speech that communicates what we're actually thinking and believing becomes a lost art.

In this lifelong enthusiasm for candor, fair play, and the well-chosen word, my father often resembled Peter Falk's Detective Columbo with a dash of Atticus Finch of *To Kill a Mockingbird*. He was entertained by the notion that "religion" is always "politics" under a different name (and vice versa), and as a conversation partner, he treated words with an amused affection and reverence, hyperaware of the many ways we go about fooling ourselves and getting fooled. Needless to say, the Bible had a lot to say about this. As a lawyer, he could appreciate the skill with which presidents could discuss the meaning of "is" or conjure up the impression that news reporters with honest questions are only out to bash, breed discontent, and aid the terrorists. He was hyperaware of all the methods whereby we can create or undo the impression of order and control through our use of language. Like Columbo, he was always respectful and generally well-mannered, even if his candor and humor invited a confession of guilt. Like Finch, he never lost a sense of the tragic as he contemplated the evil that people do and all the ways that it didn't have to go that way. Like both men, he sensed that absolute justice would leave no man standing, and he reverenced an earthbound, everyday truthfulness that makes liars of us all.

To live with this awareness, to view truthfulness not as a boasting point we have over others but as a standard that judges all our talk, is to recognize oneself as a partaker of common humanity humbly bound to the common good of attempted truthfulness. And truthfulness, like the strange world of the Bible, was a subject of which my father understood himself to be a learner, not an authority, and certainly not a professional. He was notoriously impatient with people who thought or spoke otherwise of themselves. He didn't always know how to have a conversation with people who didn't seem too well acquainted with the criminals under their own hats. Like Columbo, he was a little embarrassed for them and a little frustrated.

This frustration had a lot to do with the hope and comfort he derived from what we might term Waffle House Conversationalism, the open and folksy dynamic of people sitting and talking over food and drink in a boisterous public place. What could be more exciting or egalitarian? No appeal to the court of fact has more resonance than another, everybody has to let everybody else finish speaking, and nobody's allowed to talk too terribly loud, because people are trying to eat in peace. You're welcome to bring the Bible or the president into it, but if you don't keep your ego at a reasonable volume, you can take your conversation elsewhere. Generally speaking, no grand poo-bah gets to go completely unquestioned in the atmosphere of your average Waffle House any more than a celebrity can be privileged with a guest spot on *The Simpsons* without submitting to possible ridicule. This isn't to say that either cultural icon is completely immune to overbearing rhetoric or the herd instinct, but I can well imagine a Waffle House receptivity to Beat Generation storyteller William S. Burroughs's observation that whenever you're doing business with a self-identified "religious" person (especially those who deceive others under the added self-deception that they themselves are doing God's bidding), you'd better get it in writing. The Waffle House consensus can laugh and wince and laugh some more at a line like that, not out of a failure of respect for any faith, but out of an appreciation for Burroughs's folk wisdom (biblical, in its way) and the recognition that "Lord, Lord" can accompany any brand of American hucksterism (Matt. 7:21–22). Those who make an appeal to religion had better be ready to explain themselves humbly and carefully. Good fellowship requires good-natured self-deprecation in all our testimonials. Waffle House clientele want to hear it: the good laugh and the truthful word. They want the conversation—the more provocative the better.

Squeezed alongside polls, focus groups, and news networks' Questions of the Day ("We want to hear from YOU!"), the following is offered in the hope of igniting that fundamental ritual of a thriving democracy, the give-and-take of a lively conversation. To begin with some broad conjectures, it shouldn't be overly controversial to observe that there are toxic levels of anger and vitriol in the public square of these United States at present. Something strange is in the air. There's a lot of talk about the "true character" of America, but it is too often accompanied by raging slander against the purposes of other Americans (Red or Blue contingents) who, one would presume, might also bear a part of America's "true character," its heart and its soul. Without such obvious points on the table, what might be an interesting public debate becomes a rather cynical shouting match over who owns the copyright on the spirit of America and the most conniving carnival barkers take all. As a husband, a father, and a teacher of high school students, I am occasionally invigorated by the thought that this climate of fear and defensiveness can't go on indefinitely and that a change is going to come within my lifetime, but I've also come to believe that the madness isn't limited to the career politicians and celebrity personalities entering our lives through electronic media. An emotional disorder has settled upon us, a habitual anger that passes itself off as normalcy, and it isn't just directed at whatever Democrat or Republican might strike us an appropriate scapegoat for all of life's problems. We eventually feel it for people (neighbors, coworkers, relatives) whose opinions fail to coincide with our own and strangers who don't drive the way we think they should, an impatience that makes clear or generous thinking difficult. Like many Americans, I find myself frightened by my own anger level and the fear that there isn't anything much anyone can do about it; that I'll keep being mad at so many people (some of whom I'll never actually meet) so much of the time. I worry that future generations might be even less capable of listening kindly to people with whom they disagree or of paying attention to a story or photographic image that invites them to view their world differently. I don't want them to inherit a militant ignorance that confuses anger for strength of character or the momentary silencing of somebody else with victory.

This book is an effort in moral orientation, an attempt to make sense of the times, and, if you like, a project in anger management. It is also a call to confession and a primer in American patriotism. As the witness of the Jewish Christian tradition makes clear, the anger of human beings against what they perceive to be evil and unjust will never produce the righteousness of God (although, as anger goes, it usually *feels* terribly effective when it has hold of us), and confession is the only hope for minds whirling with contradictory impulses and filled with thoughts of courage and honor and freedom but increasingly incapable of connecting dots or adding two and two together. We're often made tired by the prospect of "politics," despairing at the mention of "religion," and hungry for a reassuring word from entertainment networks who advertise themselves as news outlets while airbrushing and organizing the real world to suit our sense of what America (our side of the divide anyway) is really about. But if we only tune in to one another to have our own thinking reinforced, are we still capable of hearing a word that doesn't assure us, in advance, that we're right and they're wrong? The biblical witness, with its contempt for fraudulence and its ongoing unmasking of all that poses as human grandeur as utter death-dealing folly, is a summons to repent (turn the mind around) and to be made whole. And lives that look to be consistently reoriented in the direction of God's good purposes (the bountiful shalom of the coming kingdom) will always maintain a redemptive tension in their relationship with the land of their sojourn, both red states *and* blue states.

To the extent that I aspire to bear witness to this coming kingdom, my hope and affection to this land and its people will not be limited to the events that formally began in 1776, the platforms of any political party, or the prerogatives of the present presidential administration. There is a call to embody a more comprehensive patriotism. Like discipleship, the practice of democracy is a widening of our capacities for moral awareness and an expansion of our sphere of respect. If we have a steadily narrowing vision of people to whom we're willing to accord respect or if the company we keep is slowly diminishing to include only the folks who've learned to pretend to agree with us, we can be assured that we're in danger of developing around ourselves a kind of death cult, a frightened, trigger-happy defensiveness that is neither godly nor, in the best sense, American.

Our preferred pundits, who many of us consult throughout the day like shots of espresso, need not define the terms by which we speak with our coworkers, and if they're making us less peaceable in the way we disagree, we might want to rethink our dependence upon them. The biblical alternative is an enlarged sense of neighborliness that strives to maintain "neighbor" as an ever-widening category. The injunction to love the neighbor in the minute particulars of speech and action has never been an easy one, but it might be the nearest and most immediate form of patriotism available to any of us. It is also the one vocation that, if neglected, will lead to the forfeiting of any and all soul.

This "Love Thy Neighbor" Stuff

With the love-thy-neighbor standard in mind, many Americans found it difficult to think hopefully of the 2004 presidential candidacy of Howard Dean when, in response to the admonition to love his neighbor, "tone down the garbage," and cease with his intense criticism of the president, he remarked, "George Bush is not my neighbor." Admittedly, it is the privilege and responsibility of every citizen to think hard about and occasionally speak instruction to each of our employees, perhaps especially those who are entrusted with our military and the way we conduct our business with the rest of the world. But Dean's statement denied the status of "neighbor" to another human being, touching a nerve that's probably more sensitive, within the American imagination, than we usually realize. Most are not yet prepared to surrender determined neighbor-love as merely a side issue (with the possible exception of a radio talk-show host or two), and we don't like having it cast aside so matter-of-factly. While Dean's campaign undoubtedly appealed to a larger vision of neighbor love than many voters wanted then or now, his point was lost in what sounded to many like an angry dismissal of whatever's left of the most practical side of the nation's Jewish Christian legacy.

In a very unfortunate choice of words, Dean suggested that now was no time to put up with "any of this 'Love Thy Neighbor' stuff." But to the thinking of many Americans, the love-thy-neighbor stuff is really all we've got. We can find ourselves idolizing celebrity, obsessing over financial prosperity, resenting Martha Stewart, and developing a crush on Tony Soprano, but a perceived assault on neighborliness by a presidential contender won't quite fly at the Waffle House. It conflicts with the myriad images many take to be the true spirit of America. And if we lose the ability to disagree without vilification, to refrain from slandering each other like poorly raised children, what hope is there for discussing real problems and real solutions intelligibly? What hope is there for democracy?

Dwight D. Eisenhower argued that without radical neighborliness and strict vigilance against our tendency to lose our heads over our strength, we run the risk of becoming just another empire. In 1961, in his farewell address, he argued that America's historical significance would depend "not merely upon our unmatched material progress, riches and military strength, but on how we use our power in the interests of world peace and human betterment . . . to enhance liberty, dignity and integrity among people and among nations."[1] As he famously put it, "the military-industrial complex," ever expanding and operating according to its own methodical, self-manufacturing logic, is a clear and present danger as it comes to alter the very structure of society and view itself as "the miraculous solution to all current difficulties." Our unquestioning faith in our own rightness and effectiveness can make us incapable of seeing that there is no military solution to a particular problem until we've given it a costly and destructive try. Eisenhower worried about what would become of a culture so altered. Absolute faith in America's not-to-be-questioned, innate goodness can create a witlessness among the citizenry, desensitize our moral imagination, and make of democracy, in Eisenhower's words, "the insolvent phantom of tomorrow."

In this sense, carefully cultivating our moral bearings in the direction of neighborly mindfulness and circumspection might be viewed as a homeland security issue. But this is no easy task when we're caught in the traffic of angry chatter, frazzled nerves, and knee-jerk reactions to sound bites that constitute an atmosphere of emotional insecurity and hypocrisy as a survival strategy. In an effort to describe and be free of it, we call this phenomenon "politics," but we probably shouldn't surrender the word so easily. Politics is how we govern

ourselves. It's the way we conduct our lives. To say, "I'm not a political person" is to claim an above-the-frayness that isn't possible for
actual human beings. In the same way, we often say, "I'm not a religious person" to avoid being pigeonholed as a fanatic or someone
who's needlessly offensive and incapable of thinking properly. But
neither religion nor politics actually work that way. And the mythology we've constructed to keep them separate in our descriptions of
ourselves and others is slowly falling apart.

When neighborly awareness and moral vigilance are considered
"nonpolitical" issues, we have no way of remembering, finding out,
or talking about what people are for. We let our leaders get away with
such nonsensical statements as "that's more about politics than policy," no longer noting that they're variations of the same words. To
be neighborly is to practice a better politics than the politics of narrowly defined self-interest. The love-thy-neighbor stuff is a different
way of being in the world and speaking to one another than is currently being practiced by the leadership of either major political party.
And what appears to be the endlessly effective nonargument of
"You're being political" (easy ammo from absolutely *any* position)
reduces us to the daily imbecility of "You're an idiot"; "No, you're
an idiot"; "No, you're an idiot."

My concern over these habits of speech can't, as far as I can tell, be
characterized as strictly liberal or conservative. But admittedly, I do
have an ax to grind concerning the slovenliness of language and loss
of coherence at work when we can no longer mean exactly what we
say or say exactly what we mean. This is a problem for democracy,
certainly, but more immediately, a vocational crisis for anyone aspiring to live a life of continuity with and faithfulness to the body politics of the Jewish Christian tradition (church or synagogue) in a land
where "faith issues" are expected to be viewed as private matters kept
far away from the increasingly antagonistic and livid public square.

God Jews Jesus Church

When Bono attempts to mobilize the American electorate toward an
awareness of the global AIDS crisis by invoking the notion of divine

judgment, when Ahmed Chalabi tells Iraq's Coalition Provisional Authority to "let my people go," when John Ashcroft declares that America has no king but Jesus, and when Martin Luther King Jr. calls the Vietnam War a "demonic destruction suction tube,"[2] it would seem strange to characterize their speech as polite appeals to someone's personal, private spirituality. King, after all, didn't simply apply a little "spirituality" to his otherwise "secular" politics. And neither Johnny Cash nor William Blake self-consciously insert the occasional "religious overtone" to give their work a little more color. The words we use to describe these appeals to the biblical witness won't work. The movement is larger than whatever category we'd like to put it in, and it happens within history. It makes history. The tradition is a patchwork of hard-won, long-learned moral insights in human affairs. And its impact can't be calculated or cordoned off to suit the interests of states or multinational corporations. One way Walker Percy devised to describe the tradition is the phrase "God Jews Jesus Church."[3] In Percy's view, it is a civilizing presence in human history, but it doesn't endorse nations or sanction the status quo. It's too big on its own, too cosmic in scope, to play chaplain to any empire. Properly understood, it won't be anybody's "spiritual component."

The question we have to bring to bear on biblical references (whether King, Bono, Chalabi, Bush, or Ashcroft) is to what extent they're faithful to the continuum described in Percy's phrase. Are they historically concurrent with the concerns of the early Christians, or are they just biblical-sounding window dressing that reassures or distracts a public easily moved by words that claim a connection to biblical tradition? With such questions in mind, this book is both a celebration of uniquely American manifestations of Jewish Christian moral insight *and* an examination of American culture in light of the tradition. And while "No other gods before me" is surely the biblical imperative against overzealous dedication to any particular tribe or nation, it is probably possible, as Tom Petty assures us, to somehow love Jesus and America too.

Enthusiasts of Jesus' gospel aren't limited to those who seek to advertise a personal association with Christianity, and it is often the case, as the Scriptures attest, that authentic faith evades any and all manufactured publicity. But these questions of historical coherence should prove relevant to anyone living within the shadow of an empire whose leaders' electability depends on the appearance of some degree of faithfulness to the God of Abraham, Isaac, Jacob, and Jesus. We do well to wonder if our leaders' God talk would make any sense to the inhabitants of first-century Palestine. It's worthwhile to ask if Jesus would say, "That's exactly what I'm talking about." These are questions that meet a Waffle House criteria of "What does this have to do with that? Is there a connection? Do the words mean what we think they mean?"

In the public discussion of any number of issues facing America, there's a sense in which Jesus of Nazareth is the elephant in the room. Could it be said that he inadvertently laid the groundwork for rock 'n' roll? Where does he fit in our foreign policy? By the logic of the Patriot Act, would he be "with us" or "against us"? While "God" or "the Almighty" is constantly invoked on any number of occasions (Grammy award ceremonies, athletic victories, political rallies), many are often hesitant to risk too specific a reference to what Jesus actually said and did, because his positions, as we understand them, might say more about preemptive strikes, unborn children, Iraqi civilians, enemy combatants, accumulated wealth, death-row inmates, and the poor than we feel we can afford to insert into a party platform or our consideration of the real meaning of success. In this, our hypocrisy might know some boundaries. We remain respectfully ambivalent concerning his teaching, though eager, as the old song has it, to be somehow washed in his blood.

"He died for me" is a moving phrase, but it's often also one way of drowning out the example of the life Jesus lived and the question of whether or not we dare to apply it to the way we conduct our own lives. There's a knee-jerk "He came to die" that avoids the specificity of Jesus' approach to enemies by suggesting that he lived the way he did so as to hasten the likelihood of getting killed for our sins. Imitating him in regard to enemy love is therefore unnecessary and maybe even naive. And yet we're nevertheless haunted by him and his explanations of what God's kingdom, civilization, and order are like. At its best, the American mind keeps constantly before itself the possibility, or rather the promise, that it doesn't yet know what civilization really consists of; that we've barely begun to hear or understand the Sermon on the Mount. There's always further to go. In the meantime America's cultural heritage might have more wisdom and insight concerning our place in history and our relationship to the coming kingdom of God than we usually assume.

Reality Sandwiches

The need to think carefully and historically about the gospel of Jesus and the perceived self-interests of the United States of America has felt especially pressing since September 11. I've long been taught that God's rule extends over our anxiety structures and our nationalisms and all of our most intricately produced delusions. But remembering as much, pointing out (out loud) that God's purposes do not inevitably coincide with whatever our nation (or any nation) decides to do (an elementary biblical notion) has become a strangely provocative idea.

For better or worse, I come from a family for whom a day without interesting conversation is not a very good day, and the notion that disagreement over "political" or "religious" issues will always end in anger and the disintegration of goodwill has always seemed like a defeat of communal possibilities, a poor witness to the coming kingdom, and bad news for the hope of democracy. Admittedly, timeliness is a factor in choosing conversational topics (at the Waffle House, the kitchen table, and elsewhere), but my faith in America's democratic culture and its draw on the biblical witness has me unwilling to believe that these questions have no place in public discourse. In an effort to sustain conversations that might otherwise end awkwardly, my wife and I began to compile a mental list of figures from American history, literature, music, television, and film that might offer redemptive stories concerning how Americans might best think about themselves. Who might we haul out, as uniquely American voices, to keep the back-and-forth going? What began with a stray Abraham Lincoln quote has become what I'd like to think of as an assemblage of American remembrance, a mix-tape to document some essential sounds, a uniquely American ebenezer around which we might try and gather our disturbed wits. We've looked hard at our American culture to see what might be teased out to speak to these strange days, surprised by some of the connections we'd forgotten about and pleased by all the history that makes us feel less lonesome as we listen to celebrity pundits sell their sense of outrage and career politicians shout like ungrown men. We've been reminded that there's more than one way to love a country, better ways to tell stories about the meaning of American civilization than many of us seem to be settling for, more to be said about "Brand U.S.A.," and much to be discovered beyond what I've thrown together in these pages.

Hermann Göring, founder of the German Gestapo, is said to have remarked, "Whenever I hear the word culture I reach for my pistol." And however it might be that close examination or appreciation of a nation's heritage (ideas, stories, preoccupations) would threaten the interests of nationalism gone murderous, my appreciative response to American culture is not intended to take a turn for the highfalutin. Somehow, examining Natalie Merchant's lyrics or reading about Eminem has never struck me as a pursuit altogether different from trying to get to the bottom of a Faulkner novel. In both cases, I'm moved by the hope that this particular someone has something interesting to say to me, and I want to hear it. I'm motivated by my assumption, hopefully not too naive, that something's inevitably there. It keeps you going.

In my own media consumption, my desire for a good story or a truthful word isn't divided between the entertaining and the informative. It's the truthful that I'm looking for (what Allen Ginsberg might call a "reality sandwich"), and the truthful account, comedy, celebration, or lamentation is good news because it acknowledges the beautiful or the tragic of lived human experience. It's gospel, because it's true. And of course, learning to desire truthfulness more than self-assurance or the facts-on-the-ground more than what would suit our preferred versions of reality is an ongoing work of prayer and confession never unrelated to listening and watching well. Truthfulness, whether in an American pop song, a poem, a sci-fi film, or a novel, will never play to our prejudices, and we shouldn't let the market divisions ("popular," "classic," or "spiritual") dictate our appreciation of what's in front of us.

It is my hope that the appearance, for instance, of Rod Serling alongside Nathaniel Hawthorne won't prove overly disconcerting. These apparent juxtapositions bring to mind a moment on *The Simpsons* when Homer informed his daughter Lisa that the whole message of *Moby Dick* could be summed up by the motto, "Be yourself." Melville had larger questions to tackle, different ones from what we're looking for in an after-school special, but his lengthy tomes aren't irrelevant to the news-of-the-day or the ways we explain ourselves to ourselves. These media are investigative. And similarly, some American popular music might afford us a deeper, darker wisdom than the notion that learning to love ourselves is the greatest love of all or that love is never having to say you're sorry.

Culture, as a descriptive term, will also have to include our Super Bowl halftime shows, Pepsi commercials that feature Bob Dole playing an avid voyeur to Britney Spears, and the ratings-sweep of *American Idol* if we're going to think truthfully about ourselves. To say the least, the less edifying aspects of our biggest cultural exports will not always fall in line with the idealistic boasting that infects our self-descriptions. But when we think beyond the market labels of "religious" and "political" or "sacred" and "secular," we will find that there are more resources for moral rearmament, edification, and expanded awareness of the sweet old world than we have thus far realized.

I Am Because We Are

In Thomas Pynchon's *Mason & Dixon,* the Reverend Wicks Cherrycoke maintains, "Remembrance belongs to the People."[4] For Cherrycoke, remembrance (telling, listening, and retelling) is the only avenue for life, liberty, and the pursuit of communal happiness. Without an awareness of all that came before, we have no legacy (American or Christian) to which we might aspire to be more faithful, no memory to be redemptively haunted by, no biblical witness to speak for or against our self-satisfied, amnesiac decisions. We will always be tempted to remember unjustly and untruthfully in an effort to protect our most flattering self-mythologies, and remembering will often be an act of communal resistance and confession. Revolution and

xxii Instead of an Introduction

reformation have always required it. And when the public's imagination is softened up, blinded by idealism, and dependent upon whatever the opinion polls tell us we're thinking or ought to think, we could probably do with a historical haunting or two.

In a slight modification of Descartes's "I think; therefore I am" (which runs the risk of an excommunicated self-understanding, alone in the false dichotomy of public/private and religious/political), African theologian John Mbiti offers the less egocentric, more family-minded "I am because we are; and since we are, therefore I am."[5] I'd also offer it as a deeply American alternative to the lesser American ideologies of "I spend; therefore I'm happy"; "I help pay for thirty-second campaign ads, so my interests matter"; and "I feel strength on account of my winning candidate." We get to practice a communal awareness and liveliness that will apply the hope of a loving future (what the believing mind might refer to as the coming kingdom of God) to whatever we call "politics" and speak comfort and truth to all debilitating despair. We get to inhabit an older, wiser, absolutely American culture compared to that which is most often televised.

Because there's more freedom for dissent than an inevitably ratings-driven television news spot can afford and more space for good-natured disagreement than we'll hear from the angry person on the car radio, the image of a Waffle House forum might again be helpful: An assortment of mostly landed immigrants (some more recently landed than others) make conversation, and to the extent that they'll see each other again the next day, the regulars might find it hard to assert that the token liberal among them doesn't believe in family values or that the resident conservative hates poor people. Their individual existences are too transparent and close to one another to allow such mean-spiritedness, even if it plays well on television and wins elections. Without a more resolute commitment to neighborliness, the huddled masses will tear each other apart.

How to Read This Book, or "Don't Shoot!"

To return briefly to the issue of a knee-jerk anger epidemic at work in America, I have an anecdotal confession that might serve as an object lesson. My wife and I have a four-year-old daughter, Dorothy Day, and like her namesake, she has a lot to say. When she senses that we're about to ask her to stop talking, the rush of things she suddenly feels compelled to talk about will often overwhelm and usually amuse everyone near at hand. We are the kind of family who often offer a prayer of thanks before meals, and while Dorothy's rush to speak freely beforehand at home serves as customary dinner entertainment, it is a slightly different matter in restaurants and with company. So recently, when Dorothy began to speak the moment we announced our intentions to pray, my wife and I immediately honed in on her, getting louder as she protested, and before we knew it, we were speaking with escalating anxiousness as we tried to impose an order and maintain the appearance of a family that prays together and stays together. We thus created a larger scene than whatever it was we'd hoped to quell. As my wife and I happened to take a breath at the same time, we eventually realized that Dorothy's intentions were not what we expected. "I have a prayer," she said. Rebuked, ashamed, and somehow strangely pleased, we bowed our heads to hear Dorothy's prayer.

In view of the reigning, obsessive haste to characterize a position as biased or agenda driven, I want to state at the outset that this work simply aspires to be a prayerful meditation upon odd times. In my conversations, I strive to keep people from too quickly jumping to a "So what you're *really* saying is . . ." and myself from an angry "What I *really* meant was. . . ." What seems to be required is an armistice in which we agree to refrain from assuming we know what's been said before we've had time to listen to or think about it. A conversation void of willful misconstruals is indeed a rare thing, but it might also be a way of witnessing to the coming kingdom. We get to have different thought habits and communication skills from that which is modeled for us on the news networks of our entertainment conglomerates, and we get to be more interested in loving well than in putting someone in their place (whatever that might mean) or making sure everyone knows (through joke, bumper sticker, or mass e-mail) where we stand.

Authentic witness, confession, and testimony might not be easily transmitted through the medium of television or easily discerned amid the slogans and mantras that characterize too much of our public discourse, but we have to try for it anyway as we attempt to make sense of our worlds. Careful thinking and listening might threaten entertainment networks that advertise themselves as news outlets while dreaming up new methods of branding our anger to better sell themselves to a fractured populace, but such care is essential for the general welfare of our American culture.

In my household, we were taught to pray especially for anyone with whom we found ourselves in passionate disagreement (notably for people in power) and to make every effort to be at peace in our relationships. But being at peace has never meant that there were some things we could never talk about or that disagreement had to end a conversation. You wouldn't know it if you only listened to the shouting matches between pundits on television and radio, but it is still possible to like someone while noting something problematic in their choice of words. You can affirm many good qualities in another person, wish them well and pray for them, and still hope that they'll never be (or will stop being) the president of these United States. We can disagree with someone's speech and practice without being anti-*them*. We get to look and listen to one another more attentively. Vigilance in both discipleship and democracy requires it. My own hope is to testify, in some small way, concerning a larger order than what we usually sense in our maddest moments, a kingdom coming (and somehow already here) on earth as it is in heaven. If I might only provoke the suspicion that there is a reality more important, more lasting, and more infinite than the cultures we inhabit and the most expensively publicized, perceived self-interest of the nation in which we find ourselves, I will be very pleased. It might be a relief. It might slow a pulse. It might even be good news.

Chapter 1

The Angel in the Whirlwind:
An Exercise in Patriotism

In view of the endless power of men to hypnotize themselves into unawareness in the presence of challenge, it may be argued that willpower is as useful as intelligence for survival. Today we need also the will to be exceedingly informed and aware.

—Marshall McLuhan

Sometimes it is not enough to correct a loss of vision or vigor; sometimes the need is to denounce idolatry or inhumanity, or to offer a hope reaching beyond present possibilities. The worst form of idolatry is not carving an image; it is the presumption that one has—or that a society has, or a culture has—the right to set the terms under which God can be recognized.

—John Howard Yoder

Have you ever ridden on a train, a mighty streamlined monster, bulleting its way over plain and mountain, and shrieking defiance to any obstacle which would hinder its progress? America is like that mighty train to me and the privilege to be a passenger on the greatest trip in all history is part of what America means to me.

—Graham Finney, What America Means To Me

I wouldn't presume to speak definitively on behalf of a dream, a spirit, a principality, or a poltergeist. But in the interest of being exceedingly aware, of expanding the sphere of sanity little by little,

1

it's often necessary to pull out the hyperbole, question the metaphors, and name the voices that get our pulses pounding. Who are we? What are we doing? Whose interests does my excitement serve? Examining our context (both geographical and historical) and seeing it clearly will involve a stretch of our powers of description and the occasional foray into the outlandish. And if we have a tendency to mistake our most cherished, insistent illusions for righteousness, integrity, or the spirit of God, there will be some states of euphoria that will only unhand us after much prayer and discernment. How else might one begin to question an image, a brand name, or a nation-state?

The apostle Paul understood the challenge. In his efforts to name the occupying forces in the bodies and minds of his community (whether the imposition of Mosaic law or the sometimes beneficial, sometimes murderous presence of a Pax Romana), he would heap words together to paint an all-purpose picture: weak and beggarly world powers, principalities, elemental forces, rulers of this age, and even angels. It's as if the new creation, the new way of being free made known in Jesus of Nazareth, has exposed whole new levels, doors within doors, of enslavement. Testing the spirits and making sense of things under the illumination of Jesus' good news (the gospel) will be an ongoing work of discernment, resistance, and faithfulness. And the convoluted, maddeningly multifaceted nature of the challenge would assume strange, new forms that the apostle could not have possibly foreseen.

What if the Gentile converts came to outnumber the Jewish believers in this fledgling community? And what if the Roman Empire decided to crown this Jewish messianic movement as its official religion with an unbaptized emperor convening councils to decide issues of doctrine? And what would become of its gospel as it was co-opted by the very powers and principalities who had executed its founder, not knowing, as he had put it, what they were doing? Do the authorities in what we consider the civilized world know what they're doing now? Do we?

I don't presume to speak definitively for the United States of America—the personality, the hope, or what President George W. Bush has referred to as "the angel in the whirlwind." But given the cultural hegemony of what we might call the American idea, the recent language (not always intended as derogatory) of an American empire, and the suggestion (as stated government policy) that a nation-state can, in the foreseeable future, "rid the world of evil," it might be an appropriate time to examine the good news of Jesus and its occasional reception within American culture.

What Is America Doing?

Something of the strangeness involved in America's relationship to the Jewish Christian tradition is captured by G. K. Chesterton's observation that America often understands itself as a nation with the soul of a church. In Chesterton's view, this isn't to suggest that America is especially faithful to any particular creed, but it's probably the only nation in the world founded on one. And most uniquely, no ethnicity, religious affiliation, family tie, or economic standing can make one citizen more American than the next. The creed won't allow it. It's self-evidently true that all are created equal, with equal access to justice. On paper anyway, Americanness is defined by this gospel. Chesterton notes that, taken to its logical extreme, this faith won't be held by pessimists or wealthy cynics and will necessarily extend its goodwill even beyond national boundaries to people outside its perceived self-interests (the foreigner, the enemy, the evildoer). He then suggests that Americans have committed themselves to something either entirely heroic or completely insane.

Stranger still, the declaration of the faith is steeped in metaphysics ("Laws of Nature and of Nature's God"), but the extension of equal rights to individuals (endowed to them, in fact, "by their Creator") doesn't require any statement of faith or doctrine on the part of the individual. Dignity is recognized within the infidel, the true believer, *and* the enemy combatant, God-given whether they like it or not. They don't even have to agree on the "God" part, and apparently the Founders didn't either.

Here, a good many of us might want to take a moment to thank God for deism and the room for creative interpretation left available by the Founders and whoever it is they had in mind when they imagined their equally created white men. The serendipitous wording would lead to all kinds of moral improvisation. James Madison would insist that an attempt to coerce correct belief is a sin against the God in whose image the not-yet-convinced neighbor is made. And Laura Bush could maintain (without a nod to any deconstructionists) that the true meaning of the Declaration of Independence was unearthed by Martin Luther King Jr.

There is a redemptive elasticity to "all men are created equal" by which it can mean more than it meant, carrying us past the trivial and tribal into better convictions than our worship of culture and homeland might, for the moment, allow. Abraham Lincoln came to view it as a stumbling block to tyranny. And as the strength of America's military presence grows beyond that of any nation in history, there's something almost salvific in the fact that, according to the document going back to 1776, no elected official or citizen is supposed to believe that some lives are more equal than others. President George W. Bush took the matter further by announcing, in his inaugural speech of 2001, that no insignificant person has ever been born. If this is a kind of creed, then a phrase like "collateral damage" is probably a kind of heresy. And the idea of America starts looking less like a mission accomplished and more like an experiment underway.

What Hath Washington to Do with Jerusalem?

If we were to draw a historical timeline of moral revelations—beginning with Moses telling the leader of his world, "Let my people go," and eventually arriving in Atlanta for Laura Bush's remarks concerning Martin King Jr. and the Declaration of Independence—we would do well to include the words of the prophet Isaiah (in the tradition of Amos, Hosea, and Micah) and his witness against social injustice under Jewish leadership; the Jewish apocalyptic of Daniel's imagining a greater government to come beyond the present understanding of Babylon; and Jesus' inaugural message in Nazareth proclaiming good news to the poor, release to captives, and recovery of sight to the blind. And of special interest to students of human rights history would be Paul's letter to the churches of Galatia in Asia

Minor. Occasionally referred to as the Magna Carta of Christian liberty, the imperatives insisted upon within the letter would guarantee that the radical politics of Jesus (once considered a sort of Jewish sect) would go global.

There are enslaving forces at work, false gods, that would categorize humans by ethnic, economic, and gender status, but in view of Jesus' lordship over all creation, these distinctions are relativized: "There is no longer Jew or Greek, there is no longer slave or free, there is no longer male and female; for all of you are one in Christ Jesus" (Gal. 3:28). To be sure, these distinctions haven't disappeared, but their legal legitimacy and cultural credibility have been undone by Jesus, and the momentarily under-the-radar, new world order to whom Paul addresses himself has no business behaving otherwise. There is another kingdom underway, and their communion is called to bear witness to it.

Similarly, a countercultural consciousness is present further back on the timeline, as Moses repeatedly reminds the redeemed of the context of the covenant: "Remember that you were a slave in the land of Egypt. . . ." The phrase appears throughout Deuteronomy, and, what is more, on setting aside the first fruits of the harvest, Israel is instructed to state aloud, "A wandering Aramean was my ancestor; he went down into Egypt and lived there as an alien" (Deut. 26:5). While not quite a wholesale affirmation of egalitarianism, a close identification with the easily exploited outsider and a renunciation of the profit-over-people ethic of Pharaoh are nevertheless nonnegotiable tenets of Israel's historical memory. Along the historical continuum we can note Jesus' privileging of "the least of these" and how the nations are to be judged by their philanthropy (Matt. 25:31–46). And closer to America's present, we might submit, as a corrective to any nativist delusions, a recitation for the historical memory of our nation of diasporas (allowing partial exemption for those of Native American descent): "A wandering immigrant was my ancestor."

But to return to Paul's explanation of Jesus' new way of being human, it's easy to forget the social novelty at work in his letter and the quiet revolution that would come of it. Within a few decades of Paul's writing, the Christian communities of Asia Minor were sufficiently widespread to come to the attention of Pliny the Younger, governor of Bythinia. In letters to the Roman emperor, Trajan, Pliny the Younger notes that the sect includes people of every class and observes, after torturing a couple of deaconesses, "I found nothing but a degenerate sort of cult carried to extravagant lengths." He also complains, "They have a passion for liberty that is almost unconquerable, since they are convinced that God alone is their leader and master."[1]

This pagan account of the visible convictions of the early Christians should give us pause as we consider how easily many Americans speak of their faith as a private, personal matter; a relationship somehow contained within the heart; an odd, airy thing called "spirituality." Such a characterization of the movement wouldn't have made much sense to the early church, and Pliny certainly wasn't describing a group of people who simply held an unconventional religious opinion or two. Admittedly, he doesn't find them especially threatening. They aren't about to take up arms against their oppressors, but they are holistically invested in a revolution. They are not apolitical. Their allegiance is to a different polity that is uniquely *for* all people. In this sense, we might think of them as *multipartisan*. They are not of this world's way of doing things, but their hope is still scandalously this-worldly. And the intensity of their passion for a socially disruptive, enduring freedom won't be diminished, divided, or conquered by the prerogatives of any government. When brought before the authorities, they matter-of-factly refuse recognition of all other gods.

Their innovative way of warring on terror and offering the embrace of fellowship across any and all communal boundaries is so inexplicably effective that the Roman historian Tacitus, offering a brief sketch of the development of this "deadly superstition," regretfully concedes that the execution of its founder was only "a temporary setback."[2] In time, the good news of this different kind of kingdom would bubble up through history like a beleaguered yet enduring effervescence eventually viewed as the common possession of anyone with an ear to hear and an eye to see. But neither Paul nor Tacitus could have anticipated a day when the Holy Roman Empire would put to the sword any who refused baptism into this "deadly superstition," or foreseen a transatlantic context in which

John Ashcroft, addressing an audience at Bob Jones University, would reference a crucified, Jewish revolutionary by insisting that, in America, "We have no king but Jesus."

The Gospel as Demythologizing Virus

Before the emperor Constantine proclaimed toleration of worship of "whatever heavenly divinity exists" in the Edict of Milan (313 CE), the difference between the good news of the empire and the good news of Jesus was reasonably clear for all interested parties. But this reversal of fortunes, accompanying Constantine's conviction that the Christian God was granting him military victories, would complicate the church's thinking on the subject of God's coming government and the governments of this world. Did this mean the prayer of "Your kingdom come . . ." had been answered? Are the principalities and powers no longer rebellious? Is this Jesus' victory over death hereby accomplished?

Then and now, thinking historically (which is to say, faithfully) involves vigilance and a mindfulness that looks critically at the supposedly commonsensical notions (or the opinion polls) of the age. This work of communal discernment will be especially crucial if it is the case that there are enslaving forces (who by nature are not gods) looking to win battles over hearts and minds. In his letter to the churches of Galatia, Paul speaks of this state of affairs as if it's obvious to anyone who's paying attention (Gal. 4:8–11). And it is to our great loss if we assume the apostle was simply imagining fiery red, sharp-eared creatures with claws and winged babies.

Somehow, the crucified Christ has conquered death, *and* the powers of darkness and delusion are still at work in the world. They lived within the tension of a new kingdom that had yet to come in its fullness, and the kingdom was the property of nobody's nation. Neither the legalization of Christianity nor the well-intentioned use of biblical phrases in televised speeches mean that God's preferred country is now on the rise. And while the polity that is the church can be pleased to reside within a culture that allows the freedom to gather and worship, the church mustn't confuse that freedom for "the glorious liberty of the

children of God" (Rom. 8:21) or the freedom for which the Christ has
set us free (Gal. 5:1), as if we have any government to thank for either.

Properly understood, the gospel of Jesus is a rogue element within
history, a demythologizing virus that will undermine the false gods of
any culture that would presume to contain it. In fact, as American history shows, the gospel itself will often instruct nations in the ways of
religious tolerance. But our understanding of the gospel is made pecu-
liarly innocuous when its witness of socially disruptive newness (in
whatever culture it finds itself) is underplayed or consigned to the realm
of "religious issues" within the private sphere. When the Bible is
viewed primarily as a collection of devotional thoughts, its status as the
most devastating work of social criticism in history is forgotten. Once
we've taken it off its pedestal long enough to actually read what it says,
how does the principality called America interpret the gospel? In an age
when many churchgoing Americans appear to view the purposes of the
coming kingdom of God and the perceived self-interests of the United
States as indistinguishable, what does faithful witness look like?

The appropriation of biblical imagery within America's cultural
consciousness is both a testimony to the tenacious inventiveness with
which the gospel takes hold *and* a stumbling block to the self-criticism
the gospel demands when it repeatedly calls a nation to repent. Tony
Campolo speaks to this tension when he describes America as possibly the best Babylon on the face of the earth, a country with much
to feel good about, but still a Babylon. There is no level of moral
grandeur to which a nation can rise beyond which the critique of Jesus
and the prophets will have nothing more to say. If it did, it would no
longer be Babylon; it would be the kingdom of God.

Jesus' announcement of a better kingdom puts any and every
Babylon on notice, and woe unto any nation that would presume itself
above the call to repentance, refusing to call into question its sacred
symbols and assuming a posture of militant ignorance. Does the biblical witness disturb the mental furniture of the average American?
Do we have the ears to hear a prophetic word? When we pray,
"Deliver us from evil," are we thinking mostly of other people from
other countries or different party affiliations, or are we at least occasionally noting the axis of evil within our own hearts and at work in
the lives of whomever we think of as "our kind of people"?

At our best, Americans are intensely awake to the contradictions we live and redemptively troubled by them. Norman Mailer has suggested that to be a mainstream American is to live the life of a walking oxymoron, to be a heart in conflict with itself, with a psyche featuring Evel Knievel on one shoulder and Jesus of Nazareth on the other.[3] Or consider Flannery O'Connor's characterization of a God-blessed, Christ-haunted American South. Many Americans seem reasonably certain that God is blessing them, one way or another, most of the time, but we're often honest enough to stop short of dragging Jesus into our rationalizations. We do what we do, for better or worse, giving thanks to God and praying for God's guidance. But I can't imagine an American politician, celebrity, or radio personality getting away with saying directly that Jesus is as America does. "Light to the Nations," "City on a Hill," and even "Freedom Itself," but push the matter too far in claiming Christ-likeness or "Operation: Infinite Justice" and somebody (hopefully not just some Muslim clerics) will complain. A folk wisdom that is inextricably a part of American culture maintains that, in Jesus, something greater than America is here.

Whatever the mythologies we use to explain ourselves to ourselves—in business decisions, ethical lapses, legal wranglings, or military interventions—there is still the WWJD-haunting, demythologizing gospel that recognizes the corruption that comes with the illusion of self-sufficiency, total power, and the suggestion (rarely spoken aloud, but often implied) that one culture might own the copyright on righteousness. Whenever the Jewish Christian tradition begins to take root in any meaningful way, interpenetrating the imagination of a people who often speak their country's name as if they were praying to it, the psychological power of patriotism is lessened or at least checked by an ancient wisdom reminding us that a nation might gain a strong economy, everyday low prices, and all the homeland security in the world and still forfeit its soul.

The Salvific Power of Self-Doubt

In this sense, the better part of American valor might be a prudential, well-learned skepticism concerning our well-laid plans. American ambition is at its best when it goes to the trouble of daring to doubt itself. We have to be at least occasionally receptive to the notion that we ourselves might sometimes be the prospering wicked of whom the Hebrew prophets speak. If we're not, we only appropriate biblical phrases (usually taken out of context) to somehow christen our already made-up minds and surround ourselves (and our listeners) with a biblical-sounding aura.

There is a tale, possibly apocryphal, of a bemused Elvis Presley sitting in front of his televisions reading the Bible. On completing 1 Corinthians 13, it is reported that Elvis had a moment of clarity, reached for a gun and began shooting the bright, electrical images making their way into his home. There's something very compelling about this scene. It's as if the man whom many would call King stepped past all that had been and would be made of his personality and all the dark stratagems of Colonel Tom Parker to render a decision. Though it has a sadness and frailty to it, the seemingly power-less gesture nevertheless delivers a bold, authoritative judgment, not without a certain dignity. With Bible in hand, Elvis compares the love that has overcome death to the brain ray that is television and all the mass hypnosis of entertainment industry it represents (inseparable as it is from the phenomenon called Elvis) and finds it wanting, deserving of, in fact, immediate execution. The King has spoken.

Or consider Abraham Lincoln, perhaps foremost among American presidents as a student of the Bible. Among his letters is a fragment entitled "Meditation on the Divine Will," written in 1862. There's something almost Melvillean (and certainly Pauline) in his identification of "human instrumentalities" that unwittingly carry out God's inscrutable will by "working just as they do." There's no sense of triumphalism or "No regrets!" or might-as-right, no particular confidence in his own decision making at the helm of one of these instrumentalities. No particular pride in being a caesar, a pharaoh, or a president if the nations, in God's hands, are just a drop in the bucket. He is only confident that, somehow, the Lord's judgments will prevail and, whatever may befall, they are true and right altogether.

He would say as much in his second inaugural address. It functions as what might be viewed as a kind of uniquely American anti-

rhetoric. It certainly doesn't inspire consumer confidence or a resolute aggression toward the enemy to imply ominously that the War
between the States is a woe given to both North and South as the woe
due the offense of slavery. Lest any "human instrumentality" insist
it's on the side of civilization in the war on chaos, Lincoln declares,
"The Almighty has His own purposes."

Malice toward none. Charity for all. Firmness in the right *as God
gives us to see the right*. Continuing the trajectory of Americans like
Presley and Lincoln, who viewed America through 1 Corinthians
13–colored glasses, I call this the Through-A-Glass-Darkly clause.
We proceed and make decisions based on our convictions of what
is right *as we understand it*. But it is not a God's-eye view. In Lincoln, we have an elected official who calls on his public to doubt
itself; to stay the course, certainly, but to maintain the modesty that
won't presume to take the will of the people (any people) for the
will of God. Pursue the right, as we dimly perceive it, with an ongoing, lively awareness of our fallibility (which is to say, our humanness) and with the humility that accompanies such awareness.
Follow your sense of right (what else can a human do?), but don't
mistake your will for the right and true judgments of the living God.
And if you see a vain delusion on the road (or on the television) slay
it. Right away.

As learners of freedom, we might come to understand that the
price of liberty is eternal vigilance. And it might be claimed that
every moral reform within American history has involved a refusal
to be bound by the oftentimes not-so-sacred intentions of our fore-
fathers and a vigilance against the tendency to worship our abstractions or to assume that whatever we feel most passionately in our
hearts is the forward movement of history. In this sense, keeping
one's head safe for democracy (or avoiding the worship of false
gods) will require a diligent questioning of any and all tribal storytellers. In an age of information technology, we will have to look
especially hard at the forces that shape discourse and the various,
high-powered attempts, new every morning, to invent public reality.
With the poignant imagery of the apostle Paul and Abraham Lincoln
in our minds, we might be better able to know a principality or a
human instrumentality when we see one.

The Light Shines in the Darkness

Our attachment to the culture into which we happen to be born is sometimes so powerful that we will resist recognizing our nation-state, tribe, or perceived master race as one human instrumentality among others. But when we find ourselves compelled to do so, we're again confronted by a demystifying, historical continuum that our divisions of church or state, sacred or secular, and religion or politics will conceal to the detriment of any hope of thinking historically. If we consult our timeline again, the account of Moses' engagement of Pharaoh on behalf of the God who heard the cry of the oppressed begins to look a lot like an early refutation of what would eventually be called the divine right of kings. And Jesus' witness before Pontius Pilate to a kingdom not of this world undoes the boasts of any kingdom that would claim superiority or unquestionable merit worthy of global dominance.

It has long been the habit of potentates to claim as much, and no consigning of religion to the private sphere protects a citizenry from the mad euphoria that demands a religious allegiance to the proclaimed interests of the state. But a culture that allows itself to be demystified by the prophetic witness of the Jewish Christian tradition will learn to doubt its own euphoria; be haunted by the Old Testament imagery of arrogant, oppressive nations at whom the Lord in heaven laughs; and note that humans whipped into a frenzy of what they take to be righteous indignation (whether by waves of nationalism, party politics, or talk radio) often have an unfortunate habit of crucifying people.

Alongside the report of Presley's lucid moment and Lincoln's subordinating all human instrumentalities (most notably his own) to the prerogatives of providence, we do well to consider a confession (affirmed by some Christian denominations in North America) that was composed as an appeal to Christian congregations in Germany in May of 1934. Repudiating the claim that any power apart from Christ should be considered a source of divine revelation (whether an elected official, the triumph of any national will, or Führer Principle), the Barmen Declaration called on German churches to "try the spirits whether they are of God" and to reject all "alien principles" or "figures and truths" that would presume to place themselves alongside (or above) the lordship of Christ. Written primarily by Karl Barth and Hans Asmussen, the document rejects the false doctrine of "other lords" and checks the totalitarian impulse of the state when it presumes absolutely or coercively to define life, liberty, and order for the human community.[4]

As we've already noted, the American mind is often already so immersed in the language of biblical imagery that distinguishing between the sayings of Benjamin Franklin and the wisdom of the book of Proverbs is sometimes a difficult task. Similarly, we are often prone to confuse Christianity with our sense of patriotism and forget that the two are not synonymous. To carefully examine our language and hold it up to careful scrutiny—with a determined awareness of our own tendency to confuse matters—is neither an unpatriotic act nor an intellectualization of what ought to be straightforward and simple. Instead, it might be better viewed as a response to the apostle Paul's admonition to "test the spirits" (as echoed in the Barmen Declaration) and the costly, patriotic practice of eternal vigilance against our tendency to hypnotize ourselves into unawareness.

Whether they assume the forms of marketeering, electioneering, or simply achieving the "right" effect with an eye on opinion polls, the words and images that come our way have power. We in the viewing audience are prone to measure a medium by how it makes us feel, instead of examining exactly what's being said and asking whether or not the words are honest, faithful to history, or demonstrably true. This is where examining content and context mustn't be dismissed as being nitpicky, argumentative, or that popular bipartisan bugbear "playing politics." It's actually the crucial discipline of both the believing church and any group who like to describe themselves as freedom loving. If we exercise no circumspection in regard to the language we use and listen to, we run the risk of being swayed by whatever false doctrines prove most emotionally intoxicating from one day to the next and whatever interpretation of current events wins the most viewers, listeners, or web page hits.

As Karl Barth noted, applying the gospel to our vision of the worlds unfolding before us will involve a yes and a no. Yes to the hope of a new day coming and the watchfulness required to see it. No to the suggestion, sometimes only dimly hinted at even to ourselves, that our own good intentions or pure hearts will hasten its coming or that we are knowers (rather than learners) of the Creator's good purposes.

In the interest of such watchfulness, let us consider the concluding words of President George W. Bush's remarks delivered on Ellis Island on the first anniversary of September 11: "Be confident. Our country is strong. And our cause is even larger than our country. Ours is the cause of human dignity; freedom guided by conscience and guarded by peace. This ideal of America is the hope of all mankind. That hope drew millions to this harbor. That hope still lights our way. And the light shines in the darkness. And the darkness will not overcome it."[5]

Like the language of the Declaration of Independence, the stated vocation of the country ("the cause of human dignity") can be interpreted to include the have-nots within America and without (with one-half of the globe surviving on less than two dollars a day, one-sixth on less than one, and the African continent ravaged by the AIDS virus in what many have called an everyday holocaust). Thus interpreted, the enormity of the challenge (a challenge, incidentally, which would probably be recognized as foundational to the witness of the global Christian church and that of the United Nations) will be impossible to overestimate. With the stakes this high, it might be important, in the interest of vigilance, spirit testing, and a reasonable self-awareness, to have in mind a confession or acknowledgement of the occasional moral lapse, on the part of the United States, in living up to this vocation.

This isn't to say that any president, commemorating a day of national tragedy, should be expected to use the opportunity to confess the nation's shortcomings. But the discerning viewer will want to keep in mind the need for confession (an ongoing part of the Christian discipline) and historical mindfulness (an obligation of citizenship). Admittedly, focus groups are likely to suggest that public officials can't get elected or remain in office without maintaining an air of insouciance regarding the less righteous moments in America's history, and career politicians have long learned how beautiful on

television is the face of the one who brings good news, announcing
peace and proclaiming news of happiness. Keeping matters clear in
our own minds and noting the possibility that some honest hearers of
these words about America's ideals might imagine Pepsi commercials, Super Bowl halftime shows, and all the ways the world might
be made safer for Wal-Mart, we can affirm these phrases for their
worth without getting carried away. Yes to the cause as stated. No to
the suggestion that anyone not yet convinced that we're living up to
it is somehow against us.

Unless we hold unwaveringly to the yes and the no of the gospel
in our listening and watching, we fall prey to a kind of confidence
game that is believed to be, for better or worse, a key part of maintaining consumer confidence and holding on to power. This is where
the pragmatic purposes of realpolitik, when successfully achieved,
inevitably appeal to what are usually described as religious sensibilities. The cause (human dignity) is described as America's "ideal,"
which, in turn, is "the hope of all mankind." "That hope still lights
our way," asserts President Bush. We hope that human dignity is a
priority in the lives of most Americans, and yet some, viewing our
culture industry, trade policies, and unilateral actions, might be forgiven for thinking otherwise. And then there is the biblical reference:
"The light shines in the darkness. And the darkness did not overcome
it" (John 1:5).

Many Americans would be pleased to hear the Bible quoted at all.
Just as many were happy to hear, in one of President Bush's State of
the Union addresses, an altered recitation of a popular hymn:
"There's power, wonder-working power, in the goodness and idealism and faith of the American people." But language that connects
American motivations with the divine Logos or Americans' presumed goodness with the blood of the Lamb who was slain should
probably give us pause. We have to examine ourselves closely whenever we try to claim (or imply) continuity with the early Christian
community. What do we mean? Are we thinking, speaking, and acting faithfully? We have to ask. Not, I hasten to add, in order to go
around policing theological correctness, but to attempt to embody a
vigilance that is both deeply Christian and, I'd like to think, profoundly American.

No Longer at Ease

Being watchful or slow to applaud a generalization shouldn't imply a failure of patriotism or anything in the way of ingratitude for the role of biblical tradition in the development of American culture. In fact, a steadfast refusal to settle for the status quo, especially in regard to whatever unfreedom we've given our allegiance to, is a fundamental part of our historical identity (think Roger Williams, Anne Hutchinson, Thomas Paine, and Harriet Beecher Stowe). As we look closer at various voices within America's literature, popular music, science fiction, and film, we will note an ongoing resistance to being entirely at ease with wherever we are, a perpetual movement forward, and a determination to speak truthfully to power, perhaps especially when that power assumes the form of an intoxicatingly unself-critical and arrogant voice within our own heads. Students of history will be especially appreciative of the morally subversive act of asking questions and the redemptively revolutionary posture required to resist mystifying forces, given our habitual preference for ignorant bliss in troubled times.

Umberto Eco once described the moment, in 1943, when he realized, as a young man, that the Fascists weren't the only political party in Italy. He suddenly began to observe how Mussolini, in power since 1922, had seemed to control the thinking of his surrounding culture at every moment and in all aspects of life, with complete power over his political unconscious. Having felt tremendous pride in his Fascist uniform, winning a writing competition for young Italian Fascists at the age of ten, and only occasionally noting another way of looking at the world via Radio London and an odd relative or two, it was quite the apocalypse to hear on the radio that Mussolini had been imprisoned by the king. As Eco tells it, "Like a butterfly from a chrysalis, step by step I understood everything. . . . It was inconceivable that this man, who since my birth had been a god, had been kicked out; I was astonished, amazed, amused." And in one mad moment, "I discovered the meaning of plurality, democracy and freedom."[6]

Astonished, amazed, and amused. If I might be allowed the pleasure of having it both ways, I'd like to suggest that America, mythologically speaking, might be helpfully viewed as both the most self-consciously anti-Babylonian world power in history *and,* given its current status as the sole world power exclusively positioned beyond the bounds of international accountability, a power most at risk of being completely deaf to the prophetic witness *against* our inner Babylon. We're liable to search the Scriptures and quote them mostly in whatever manner will best suit our sense of innate goodness (public or private), so certain that the Bible speaks for us (and we for it) that we become contrition proof. And yet we also have a heritage (Christ-haunted, if you like) that is *astonished* at how absolute power so subtly corrupts absolutely, *amazed* at the self-justifying logic that accompanies our moral ruin, and *amused* over how thinly our self-congratulatory rhetoric conceals an impenetrable ignorance. Too noisy an assertion of America's moral grandeur and superiority might occasionally betray a nagging doubt or two. And it is the doubt concerning our own loudest and brightest publicity that might keep the rest of the world looking hopefully on our broadcasts.

As a younger man, I once had an astonishing, amazing, and amusing moment of my own in a Belfast pub after watching Clint Eastwood's *Unforgiven* (1992). I'd been working with the YMCA in Northern Ireland for a few months, and for the first time in my life I'd experienced my Americanness as a distinguishing feature. It was strange to be referred to as an American (by way of description), occasionally unsettling even, but also extremely entertaining. It disturbed an ease that I hadn't known was there. The folks with whom I'd gone to the cinema were an international gathering, and all agreed that this was Eastwood's finest work yet, a western to end all westerns (The Kid: "He had it coming." Eastwood: "We all have it coming, kid."[7]), and possibly the best film Cormac McCarthy never made.

I did have a slight qualm, however, concerning one of the final scenes, in which Eastwood's protagonist, having wreaked vengeance on all parties involved in the murder of Morgan Freeman's character, cries out, like a mad cowboy Lear, that he will hunt down and slay all evildoers and their wives and their children in his battle against injustice. I thought it a bit much to have an American flag flying in the background during the speech. It's not as if America is the only country guilty of falling prey to the myth of redemptive violence, I pointed out, and while I believed that Eastwood's direction was, otherwise, completely brilliant, this struck me as overkill, a slight misstep in the direction of the preachy.

An Ulsterman, slightly older than I, laughed at my fastidiousness. "But that flag's everybody," he protested. "It's shorthand for human nature. It *is* redemptive violence and freedom and pride and all that. Clint's all of us. The flag too." Most nations had been made to drink the wine of the wrath of America's fornication for many years now. It's everybody's. Didn't I know it? And with this, I began to suspect, probably for the first time, that I'd lived and breathed and grown up within a metaphor, a citizen of what, for much of the world, is a very big idea that *obviously* isn't always true to its bolder claims of freedom and justice for all. It's a great big, human experiment in democracy. What's the big deal in acknowledging as much? Nobody's perfect, right? We all want to win. We all get carried away. We're all only human. It began to dawn on me that I'd come from the land where most of the big-budget action films and popular sitcoms took place, and I felt like I'd just been stopped short in the middle of a sales pitch. Not long after that, I could hardly believe my good fortune as I eagerly attempted to explain the concept of Manifest Destiny to an inquisitive Frenchman. He nodded knowingly as I struggled to be a good commercial on behalf of my country, but I eventually realized that, even though Manifest Destiny was an indisputably interesting notion to him, he'd actually only asked me to describe Memphis, Tennessee.

Around this time, it began to occur to me that being properly introspective and self-critical concerning America and less defensive when someone good-naturedly doubts its publicity might be one way of being more Christian, more globally minded, and probably even more patriotic. Trying to explain America outside of America, only to find that, for better or worse, America had been on everybody's minds already for some time, was a deeply disconcerting experience. I hadn't given a lot of thought to international opinion. It was as if I'd emerged from an alternative reality (a la *The Truman Show*). When a German friend asked, "What do Americans think of Germany?" I forget how I responded exactly, but I remember that the first not-so-proud thought in my mind was that, generally speaking, we don't.

The Tonto Principle

Since then, this astonished, amazed, amused sensibility has come to inhabit my conversations, my prayers, and my reading of the Bible. It has become a moral imperative, in fact, that's been easier to keep in my mind as my communal network of friends inside and outside of America has grown and deepened. I certainly mean more than I used to when I use the word *Christianity* (as well as *America*), and I suspect the activity of remaining awake to the wider world is an ongoing work involving the communal discipline of discernment within any culture. Needless to say, the events of September 11 brought new challenges and new conversations.

The e-mails, phone calls, and visits continued. And the much-talked-about outpouring of international solidarity was also made manifest in my friendships. In time, however, it became necessary to clarify (or at least offer a word of reassurance concerning) the durability of these relationships, perhaps especially with those who think of themselves, to any degree, as my sisters and brothers in Christ. Over the last two thousand years, millions have been admonished by the words of Jesus concerning God's new world order: "He that is not with me is against me" (Matt. 12:30; Luke 11:23). My overseas friends who aspire toward Christianity are in general agreement that keeping this proclamation in mind is an ongoing aspect of the confession required of discipleship. What are we to make of it, then, in view of our international communion, when President Bush, invoking the language of Jesus, draws a rhetorical line in the sand that proposes to define international relations: "You're either with us or against us in the fight against terror." As the principle was repeated and broadcast, eventually becoming a kind of mantra (all the more authoritative sounding for its seeming resonance with Jesus' words), it had to come up in my correspondences eventually. Could one be against terror (according to most Americans) without agreeing with the Bush administration's response to what it terms "terror"? Could the Associated Press? Could Democrats? Could the average Palestinian? Could the rest of the world? Does the Pentagon own all abstract nouns? And who does the royal "us" refer to? What becomes of baptism? Does it include you and your family?

Sort of. And if it isn't clear already, the book you're holding is, in no small way, a child of these conversations and their tangents and an effort to cobble together an "us" (noteworthy agents of the free throughout American history; friends of freedom, if you will) especially worth looking into. But concerning the "us" part of any culture's "with us or against us," many have been helped (myself included) by Stanley Hauerwas's explanation of the Tonto Principle. As the story goes, the Lone Ranger and Tonto once discovered themselves to be in a very tight spot with twenty thousand Sioux surrounding them on every side. Taking note of their predicament, the Lone Ranger turns to Tonto and says, "This looks pretty tough; what do you think we ought to do?"—to which Tonto replies, "What do you mean 'we,' white man?"[8]

As a Christian ethicist, Hauerwas has remarked that one of the biggest challenges of his career is convincing the church (whose ethos will be very different from that of any nationalism or movement of the present age) of how crucial it will be to imagine more carefully and define its "we" impulse. Just as the Barmen Declaration offered a word of clarifying resistance in the psychological warfare of the Nazi era, an ongoing application of the Tonto Principle will be necessary in any effort to cultivate, within one's culture, an awareness (an identity) as a people of new creation more radically catholic, which is to say, more universal, and more caught up and entrenched within the tribe-transcending, utterly international body of Christ.

But as the church has long understood, this can get a little complicated. In an age of totalitarian consumerism—with news networks vying for higher ratings with whatever viewers can be taught to settle for in the way of incantations and imagery and personalities presenting themselves as independent thinkers to an audience increasingly incapable of associating cause with effect—knowing how to feel, how to think historically, and how to exist within a community becomes an urgent and powerfully demanding task for the church. The call to worship, the people of God will understand, does not limit itself to what we normally think of as religious assemblies. Many and various calls will be transmitted via every kind of electronic media. And given their market research, focus groups, and the dire need to move units, the calls will be very persuasive. The church must not be guided by whatever ideology or campaign happens to have the upper hand in whatever nation-state we happen to be born in. The biblical admonition to "test the spirits" is well aware of the intense emotional appeal and high-tech hocus pocus that exhausts our minds, but vigilance and resistance have never been possible apart from communal discernment. We have everything to lose by uncritically embracing the best-selling, cartoonish versions of complex realities.

Sir, We Have a Situation Here

In an interesting take on the meaning of patriotism, Karl Barth once suggested (around the time of the Barmen Declaration) that true loyalty to one's land cannot be known apart from the example of Jesus. Apart from exemplifying a higher and more grounded Christology than most have thought to imagine, this suggestion is also an illuminating way of thinking about Jesus' vocation to Israel and other people groups living under Roman occupation. Consuming media in North America, talking about it, praying, reading, listening, and attempting to think historically will require thinking hard (and probably thinking anew) about what we mean when we refer to Christianity or, more specifically, what we have in mind when we use the word *gospel*. And if Jesus himself followed Jeremiah's call for Jewish diaspora to seek the welfare (the shalom) of his culture (Jer. 29:7), what might it mean to stand within his movement (once termed "the Way") as a citizen of the land called America in these very odd times?

Jesus was born into a tribe that, from long before his birth and long after his death, struggled to maintain faithfulness to Yahweh despite constant persecution. If the fair and balanced scribes of Jesus' time had borrowed the language of twenty-first-century news media, they might have referred to their plight as one of "freedom under attack." He was a second-class citizen. In the jargon of "good vs. evil" he'd have had no trouble recognizing the "evil" ones, namely Rome and its puppet governments, which, in his case, took the house of Herod and their cronies. (N. T. Wright has suggested that Herod the Great has a contemporary parallel in Saddam Hussein, except that Herod never broke away from his creators so boldly as to provoke their wrath.) According to the Gospel of Matthew, Jesus was born under a death sentence. He would have heard of numerous insurrections performed on behalf of his people having been violently put down, often leading to numerous crucifixions, and of little men being erased all the time. In an effort to create a familiar context for my students, I've suggested that Jesus lived in a situation similar to that of Mel Gibson's characters in both *Braveheart* (1995) and *The Patriot* (2000). And the opportunities of what we think of as life and liberty available to him were, perhaps in an even more severe way, limited.

It was in this context that Jesus announced his "good news." When Americans refer to the gospel, they might be speaking of the idea that, if you believe a certain list of true propositions, you'll go to heaven when you die. Or they might be suggesting that if you accept Jesus as your "personal savior," you'll find it easier to overcome addiction, guilt won't be the problem that it used to be, and you'll now be the bearer of a secret password ("Jesus") that will keep you out of Hell. From the *Left Behind* point of view, the good news of the gospel can mean that when you give intellectual assent to the claim that Jesus is God, you become one of the people who'll disappear before the trouble starts. While all of these understandings of the gospel gain ground throughout America and the rest of the world (perhaps even assuming the form of a uniquely "Americanized" Christianity), it's important to note that none of them would have made the slightest bit of sense to Jesus' hearers. They were under the foot of an oppressive regime, and Jesus' announcement meant, if it was deserving of the title of "good news," that things were about to turn around, that the kingdom (the rule) of God was at hand. They understood that he was inaugurating a movement that, for starters, was "good news for the poor" (Luke 4:18) and bad news for the powerful on their thrones and those who are proud in the thoughts of their hearts. When we read the prayers of Mary and Zechariah in the first chapter of Luke's Gospel, it's hard to miss the call, echoed throughout the Hebrew Scriptures, for regime change.

Did this mean that Jesus was preparing to retaliate? It seems apparent that many of his followers thought so. Their way of life had been under attack as long as any of them could remember, and there were at least a few Zealots among them who, by definition, were set on armed revolution. He had to rebuke them for misunderstanding his movement when they expressed their desire to call down fire upon the opposition. And as Peter listened to Jesus' repeated insistence that he would be arrested, tortured, and killed, Peter made it clear that he would gladly kill and be killed to prevent such a fate from befalling such an innocent as Jesus. On hearing this, Jesus didn't turn to Peter and, with a somber bow, declare, "Praise and honor to you, great warrior, for offering to kill on my behalf." On the contrary, we have the devastating "Get behind me, Satan," in which Jesus recognizes, in Peter's impulse to defend his lord with lethal means, another manifestation of the Tempter in the wilderness.

The defining ethic of Jesus' movement (his gospel) was at least as difficult for his generation to accept as it is for ours: "Love your enemy"; "Bless those who curse you"; "Do good to those who hate you." The scandalous ineffectiveness of such commands, given the climate of fear and hatred, would have been met with the same hostility they're met with today. He might have been told that evildoers won't respond well to such sensitivity. And doubtless, many would have suggested that Jesus was failing to live up to what was required of any decent, upstanding member of his tribe. They might have called him a self-hating Jew. But more than anything in the way of yet another nationalist movement, he was inaugurating a new understanding of effectiveness, a truly revolutionary revolution, a new definition of the good, a tribe to end all tribes, a new way to be human. And as news of his resurrection would attest, his way was the way everlasting, the path that would endure.

This newness isn't a byproduct of the gospel. According to the New Testament witness, Jesus' way *is* the gospel, the good news for all nations, for every tribe, now and forever. And the body of Christ is a new nation, a royal priesthood that seeks to embody the more excellent way. When the church is the blind, uncritical endorser or "spiritual" chaplain of whatever the nation decides to do, it has largely renounced its vocation as the body of Christ. It is neither the salt of the earth nor a light to the nations. And it has traded its worship of a crucified Jew for a devastatingly tribal idolatry.

To return to Jesus' historical context, it's admittedly difficult for many Americans to sympathize. Most of us are not in the position of a Jew in first-century Palestine whose status is essentially that of a slave (Phil. 2:7). For many in the world, struggling to survive under tyrannical regimes with Normal Trade Relations or Most-Favored Nation Status with the United States or barely surviving under the less life-sustaining end of a global trade agreement, America is undoubtedly Rome. Questions to keep ever before us are, How do we follow the Jewish revolutionary and his countercultural movement, live along his continuum two thousand years later ("He who is not with me is against me"), and bear faithful witness to the kingdom to which he invites us and for whose coming we are taught to pray? How do we go about participating in this story? If Karl Barth is to be believed, these are not side issues in our efforts to be true, whatever that might mean, to the country (or empire) in which we find our-selves, and as Dietrich Bonhoeffer understood, patriotism can be a very lonely occupation.

The book of Jeremiah offers an account of a maddening situation. Jeremiah is told that he was set apart in his mother's womb to declare God's words. He is also told that no one will listen to him and that he will be reviled. He is told to announce the destruction of Judah, which is the result of their whoredom, the exchange of their glory for that which doesn't profit. Devastation will come, but he is also called to announce restoration, the forgiveness of sins, and hope for the hope-less. The book is a record of his struggle with a God who tells him to condemn his people, grieve for them, pray for them, plead with them, plead for them, and treasure them. When we note Jesus' similar voca-tion toward his own people, a vision (a beginning anyway) starts to develop concerning what it might look like to embody or practice the aforementioned movement within the world called America.

Hazarding the Infinite

Shortly after September 11, Donald Rumsfeld announced, "We have two choices, either to change the way we live, which is unacceptable, or change the way they live." After applying the Tonto Principle, I'm able to remind myself, in the spirit of Abraham Lincoln, that I shouldn't be too quick to place the Almighty on one side of the paradigm just proposed. It occurs to me that America's way as the nonnegotiable future for everybody else in the world isn't necessarily suggesting a radically new state of affairs. In the months following September 11, with America being referred to repeatedly as "freedom itself" and all decisions placed under the umbrella of the war on terrorism as a matter of never-to-be-questioned good versus irredeemable evil, I wondered how many people around the world viewed America's trade and foreign policy as an ongoing attack on "freedom itself." I recall one of Jesus' interlocutors referring to Jesus as "good" as well as Jesus' response: " 'Why do you call me good? No one is good but God alone' " (Mark 10:18).

Of goodness and freedom, righteousness and liberty, we are not knowers, and the struggle to differentiate between what is now and then foisted on our minds as America's best interests and the prerogatives of the kingdom of God will require keeping this confession in our minds. The church doesn't recognize itself as the copyright owner of God's kingdom or freedom or Jesus' lordship, but it does hope to learn the ways of God's already-underway civilization and, guided by the Holy Spirit, bear witness to God's future in the rebellious present. Using the language of Jesus' great commission to his Jewish disciples to go out and disciple all nations, Woodrow Wilson maintained that the United States of America itself was created by God "to show the way to the nations of the world how they shall walk in the paths of liberty." He went on to say, "It was of this that we dreamed at our birth."[9] While Wilson failed in his efforts to rally the country behind the League of Nations, it isn't necessarily a naive or arrogant gesture to hope that a human instrumentality might occasionally seize a vocation beyond that of collective self-aggrandizement and profit over other people.

This is a good hope. And every once in a while in the histories of communities and nations, it is powerfully realized. But staging it, conjuring it up in a media blitz, or mistaking a successful marketing campaign for a mission accomplished is a different matter from really calling it out, embodying it, and tying the hope down to the facts on the ground. Within the Jewish Christian tradition (the continuum that Walker Percy summed up as "God Jews Jesus Church"[10]), the hope is accompanied by ongoing confession and lamentation concerning the daily failure (in general and in particulars) of human beings to live up to the hope of real live humanism. And the rhetoric of self-proclaimed righteousness (from Pharaoh's hardened heart to "Power of Pride" bumper stickers) is undermined and mocked from Genesis to Revelation. One would think that the enormous, mostly agreed-on, historical missteps in American history and church history would have us speaking with a bit more modesty or with some measure of apprehension concerning our karmic account, conceding that history can't be controlled and renouncing, once and for all, our pretensions toward omnipotence. As students of the witness against Babylon, Rome, and any and all antichrists, we should note how easily an emotional fantasy can become a kind of phantasm with a life all its own (test the spirits) and let the biblical witness warn us against impersonating a race chosen by God.

With these hazards in mind, we now turn to what might be viewed as recurring heresies within American culture (though not peculiar to it) while also examining some uniquely American criticisms of and correctives to these heresies. As we speculate concerning the purposes of God's kingdom in all of this, it shouldn't be overly controversial to observe that these purposes will surpass the righteousness of the Pharisees, the Democrats, and the Republicans. When viewed alongside what we believe we perceive of this coming, already/not-yet kingdom, America's efforts at self-improvement, law and order, and the uprooting of every perceived threat will often have the appearance of a carefully orchestrated mass delusion. For a nation, being quick to admit as much, not slow to repent or righteous in its own eyes, will probably be as close as any human instrumentality (or principality or power) can come to glory.

Chapter 2

Song of Ourselves: Narcissism and Its Discontents in a Bipolar Nation

Reuben's secret thoughts and insulated emotions had gradually made him a selfish man, and he could no longer love deeply except where he saw or imagined some reflection or likeness of his own mind.
—*Nathaniel Hawthorne,* Roger Malvin's Burial

So come out of those ugly molds and remember good is better than evil because it's nicer to have around you. It's just as simple as that.
—*William S. Burroughs,* The Ticket That Exploded

This train is known as the Black Diamond Express to Hell. Sin is the engineer, Pleasure is the headlight, and the Devil is the conductor.
—*Rev. A. W. Nix,* Black Diamond Express To Hell—*pt. 1*

*I*f there's ever a made-for-TV movie about what TV has made of the American mind, an incredibly good line or two will probably go to onetime president of CBS News Fred Friendly. Often referred to as the other half of Edward R. Murrow, Friendly was an indefatigable journalist who believed that his vocation (and that of any news organization) was to provide individuals with information on which they can actually act. What is more, he believed that the storytellers of media should resist making up people's minds or shaping their desires (a conflict of interest, needless to say, if high ratings are the only possible bottom line) and strive instead to tell it like it is in such

27

a way that the viewer is drawn into the agony of having to make a decision. According to Friendly, the journalist's job is "to make the agony of decision-making so intense that you can only escape it by thinking." Given his view of the crucial role of media within a functioning democracy, there was a witness-bearing consistency in his decision to resign his position, in 1966, when network executives canceled live broadcasts of testimony on the subject of Vietnam before the Senate Foreign Relations Committee, opting instead to air sitcom reruns.

Like Rod Serling, Friendly believed that television was an almost unimaginably powerful tool for positive social change, but it also had the potential to become nothing more than a hi-tech totem pole of mass hypnosis that could serve the ends of multinational corporations and the nation-states that serve them, with airtime handed over to whatever forces will pay the most to colonize brainspace. We get what we pay for, and concerning the pattern of most-viewed programming turned most-lucrative advertising space, Friendly eventually observed that "television makes so much at its worst that it can't afford to do its best." He would later pine for the days when news programs would regularly feature people lost in thought or ready to admit that a particular issue would require more thinking before a comment would be prudent. In Friendly's ideal future, television might have often featured the rare happening of people actually changing their minds or conceding a point in a conversation. But it wasn't to be. So much for Socratic dialogue beaming its way into a nation's living spaces.

Freedom-loving Americans

Advocates of civil discourse as an indispensable aspect of a stable democracy will want to affirm the legacy of Fred Friendly. But this is an especially difficult affirmation to keep a grip on in a mass-media age of everything all of the time. The comedian Jon Stewart notes the irony of what is ostensibly a news program calling itself "Crossfire." As a military term, it aptly captures the danger bystanders will find themselves in when two tribes go to war, but, in this case, the "crossfire" is what viewers are urged to call "news," as two personalities shout at each other, willfully misconstruing one another's positions while the studio audience applauds. Friendly hoped for an American culture that would learn to enjoy well-articulated argument, capable of distinguishing between information and accusation, while eager to be entertained and challenged by the complexity of the workaday world.

But we've found ourselves in a cultural climate that appears increasingly unlikely to promote the skills required to think coherently about ourselves or to properly converse with each other. The trouble with a sound-bite culture that resents complexity and lacks the patience to listen to (or read) any account of people, places, or events that doesn't somehow prove we're in the right is that it eventually becomes a sort of feedback loop playing over in our heads even when we aren't tuned in to the television, radio, or computer screen. Our minds become populated with the slogans, short answers, talking points, and clichés that made us feel strong and in control when we heard them, and we only like to hear them reaffirmed.

Sooner or later, we avoid the company of people who don't buy into our chosen slogans or respond favorably to our mass e-mails, and we unknowingly define our community by the people who agree with us or who have at least learned to dutifully avoid particular topics in our company. Tragically, it can become what we mean when we think of friendship. We become our own death cult (or target market), and we feel most alive when we listen to talk-radio personalities who tell us how to feel.

If we're going to focus on the family, embody the church's vocation by way of a countercultural lifestyle, or sustain the necessary skills to respond redemptively and without anger to a difference of opinion, we will deny the dominant paradigms of the feedback loop the status of social acceptability. Ancient wisdom tells us that it's the insane person who can't change his mind and won't change the subject, but somehow, popular media culture in America, inevitably driven by viewer ratings, has reached a fever pitch that views thoughtfulness as weakness and a changed mind as treachery. Militant ignorance passes itself off as integrity, and our habits of mind learn to dismiss illuminating fact and testimony with the nonargument of "bias" (whether liberal, conservative, or anti-American) or "politics" (any interest that threatens my own).

To be human is to be biased, and to be a citizen is to be political. Impartial judgment is a hope, rather than a boast, for those of us who only see through a glass darkly. Like humility, it probably isn't the kind of attribute someone can possess knowingly. Human beings spin whenever they speak, and the only No Spin Zone, according to biblical witness, is the coming kingdom of God. If we claim to be without spin, we lie to ourselves. We might just as well claim we have conquered anger or selfishness or finiteness. But advertising language (which, by definition, misleads) is not accountable to confessions of mortality and can decree itself fair and balanced with an audio/visual blitzkreig. It can present itself as being without spin and is more than able to cast the first stone. With the backing of a media conglomerate, pundits can vouchsafe a sense of false community and sound mindedness on anyone who gives the Amen to their view of the cosmos. The listener gratefully reciprocates the passing of the peace of mind (I think what you think), a commodity that sells itself.

If we take Lincoln's meditations on divinity (Your pounding pulse is not the Holy Spirit) and Presley's cryptic triumph over television as exemplary moments in Americans' struggles to more accurately perceive ourselves and our place in the world, we might say we're at our best when we're at our most bewildered, when we're eager to have our made-up minds undone by new and better testimonies, when we want truth spoken to our own power, and when we're afraid of our own anxious tendency to dismiss information that might make us think twice about ourselves. Self-congratulatory paranoia might sell and, to some minds, popular witlessness might even strengthen the economy, but a nation of psychopaths won't go far in projecting democratic values on the world. America as a commodity becomes less appealing to the global village when America presents itself as a creature that only listens to itself. It's hard to appreciate a service provider that denies all negative feedback in advance of hearing it.

With this in mind, our ability to feel disaffected with the self-referential stories we've clung to, discovering (blessedly) that we don't know the half of it, might be the nearest available avenue toward patriotic acts. At the very least, thinking freely, listening

humbly, and imagining differently shouldn't be viewed as side issues ("spiritual," "personal," or "intellectual") when trying to judge the state of the union. In fact, getting this work right in our relationship with the other 96 percent of the world's population might be the most pressing issue of national security.

Still, Small Voice

The hours we spend in our automobiles as a captive audience to the princes of the power of the airwaves and the ease with which we can convince ourselves we've scored a point in a debate with a keyboard or a click of the mouse have left many Americans in a lonely bind. Tragically, our yearning for community makes us especially vulnerable as host bodies for whatever force might hold a megaphone closest to our ears, and the hype that gets hold of us won't generally make us more loving in our responses to friends and family. We're free-floating, unnerved, and easily susceptible to multimillion-dollar, manufactured versions of reality.

On top of this, we have that much-touted notion of American individualism that, in one sense, is inseparable from the Jewish Christian tradition. The creed (no insignificant person was ever born) exalts the human being as the infinitely valuable bearer of God's image and eventually deems every person as so endowed with dignity that all are to be accorded, with all deliberate speed, rights. But as thinkers like Alasdair MacIntyre, Robert Bellah, and Stanley Hauerwas have effectively demonstrated, this rights-talk, divorced from its historical moorings and any awareness of the cultures that converted pagan devaluing of humans to a lifting up of humans as divine, can make people rather nasty, brutish, and blissfully egotistical, with little understanding of the humanism they've inherited at great cost. Humans are more than creatures that walk around on two legs and have rights, but the ways we've imagined a division of public and private, sacred and secular, make it easy to forget that human rights weren't discovered by statesmen or scientists. Humans are worthy of food, shelter, education, and trial by jury, but modern-day liberalism doesn't always acknowledge that it was primarily the creative moral

witness of the church in history (St. Patrick, Erasmus, Wilberforce, Martin Luther King Jr.) that taught the powerful to believe as much.

The exaltation of the rights-bearing individual, supposedly held up by its own strength of individual spirit, leads to a hopeless privileging of personal fantasy as the definitive take on reality. Mistaking the still, small voice in our minds for a divine whispering isn't a uniquely American heresy, but combined with the deifying of personal intuition, passion, or whatever it is we might mean when we talk about the ineffable virtue of following our hearts, one prevalent understanding of personal strength becomes an insane sense of personal infallibility. Being true to oneself, in the most vapid sense, might simply be a matter of being true to one's endlessly self-justifying ego.

In *Habits of the Heart,* Robert Bellah and his colleagues document one particular form of American self-worship and identify it as "Sheilaism," the professed, private faith of a young nurse named Sheila Larson (a pseudonym) who named her most consistent religious conviction after herself. She's quick to point out that she believes in God, but she isn't a religious fanatic: "My faith has carried me a long way. It's Sheilaism. Just my own small voice."[1] Self-love and being gentle with herself concerning possible shortcomings are her exclusive creeds. The authors don't question that Sheila has had experiences with a living God, but it does seem clear that God, viewed through the lens of rampant Sheilaism, can become nothing more than "the self magnified."[2]

I hasten to add that this brand of egotism isn't the sole property of any particular political party, economic class, or group. "I believe *in my heart* . . ." is a stunningly effective phrase in the perception of the American public, if the polls are to be believed, and "he believes in himself" is a strangely persuasive bit of nonsense that, nevertheless, appears to buttress the occasional approval rating. Presidents can refer to their "heart of hearts" and talk about the unique truth of what's deep down in their hearts as if feeling something deeply is an argument in itself. G. K. Chesterton famously observed that the highest concentrations of people who most intensely believe in themselves are to be found in mental institutions, but, taking a page out of Joseph Goebbels's notes, we can be assured that unquestioning self-confidence still somehow feelingly persuades. A firm hold on one's

personal rightness is a major tenet of high-profile American leaders whether refusing to look at the facts of an arms-for-hostages trade, question the justice of preemptive strikes, or speak candidly of what was meant by talk of "that woman."

A Personal, Private Faith

Like other Americans, our presidents often appear to embrace a variation of the Quaker doctrine of the Inner Light of Christ, but with the absence of anything in the way of communal discernment or accountability that might call into question the confidence with which a person heeds the voice in one's heart. "Personal religious experience" seems to settle the issue of religious allegiance in voters' minds, even as actual allegiance to any visible community of faith (present or past) is viewed as political suicide. John F. Kennedy and John Kerry can claim affiliation with the Roman Catholic church while assuring the people that no church teaching or papal decree will have any actual effect on their decision making. And in what we shouldn't assume was a calculated move, then-Texas governor George W. Bush wins the approval of millions by citing "Christ" as his favorite political philosopher. Needless to say, an explanation on the specifics of how his foreign policy or his position on capital punishment will line up with the Sermon on the Mount (political philosophy, after all) is not forthcoming, but this is well in keeping with the mass-market version of American Christianity. The actual politics of Jesus aren't usually included in a nation's God-talk. How is it, then, that Jesus influences? "Because he changed my heart." When his interlocutor hints that the American people might desire a little more elaboration, he smiles and observes, "If they don't know, it's going to be hard to explain."

And he's right. It's what millions of Americans are referring to when they say that they know or that they've "got" Jesus as their savior. I don't mean to imply disingenuousness on the part of anyone when I suggest that this way of talking isn't necessarily faithful to the traditional Christian confession. Harold Bloom has suggested that "knowing" Jesus, believing yourself to have a one-on-one relationship with him (unmediated by tradition; "in the garden alone"; impossible to explain to anyone who doesn't know him like you do), is a recently developed form of gnosticism that is probably the real, most-often-practiced, American religion.[3] Minus the obligation to aspire toward continuity with a historic, visible, practicing community (based in some recognizable fashion on what Jesus of Nazareth said and did), we're left alone with what we believe in our hearts our personalized Jesus is telling us. The nonpolitical, fully spiritualized Jesus is on the rise in America.

As a cautionary measure against our tendency to tell ourselves the Jesus in our heart of hearts is telling us to do whatever we've already decided to do or that the Bible somehow buttresses whatever we feel is right, the Christian prayer of confession affords us the opportunity to recognize ourselves as fallible discerners of whatever it is the Spirit is saying to the churches. Trying to be faithful to that word, perceived with fear and trembling, is what the church does. But to the Christian mind, the individual human heart, far from having a direct line to God, is, to borrow the language of Jeremiah, both deceitful above all else and desperately wicked. The word "Christ" (a title, and not Jesus' last name) can't simply be inarguable shorthand for a personal sense of rightness, as if there's nothing to talk about and nothing to be explained. To say that Jesus is the Messiah is to say that his politics goes. It can't just be a codeword for "in the know" concerning the importance of a certain kind of "spiritual component" that will have little or nothing to say on the subject of the poor, death-row inmates, or evildoers (nonspiritual issues?). Is our talk of our knowledge of Christ divorced from an apprenticeship to his way of doing things? When we say we know him (or that someone else doesn't) are we making reference to the historical Jesus or are we simply talking about some well-meaning, inarticulate heart longing? This is why communal accountability, discernment, and confession of sin will, traditionally, *save us from* the tyranny of a "personal, private faith" and the clear and present dangers of Sheilaism.

But liberalism is tailored to suit this particular heresy, and it is the air we breathe. It so informs our thinking that it will sound completely crazy for anyone to suggest, as Hauerwas did, that one pressing question in regard to Bill Clinton's misleading statements about his extramarital relations isn't so much the issue of impeachment but whether or not his church should discipline him, for his own emotional health, with at least momentary excommunication. And when asked about his life as a man of prayer and the decision to go to war, nothing will sound amiss when President Bush responds with the following:

> I don't bring God into my life to be a political person; I ask God for strength and guidance; I ask God to help me be a better decision. The decision about war and peace is a decision I made based upon what I thought were the best interests of the American people. I was able to step back from religion, because I have a job to do. And I, on bended knee to the good Lord, asked Him to help me to do my job in a way that's wise.[4]

As a testimonial, this is a powerful portrait of the liberal view of religion, and it should be familiar to all of us. There is a pathos at work, and it's reflected in the way we balance our jobs with our Sunday morning faith, the way we do business, the way we often feel obliged to put our faith to the side when we're buying and selling, the way we go about being realistic. This is the struggle of vocation, of faithfulness to a job with certain demands that might not coincide with the language usually associated with religion, of a human heart in conflict with itself. The view of God as a nonpolitical being that we can bring in for wisdom and comfort *and* keep respectfully separate from our business, our "job to do," is a view held by Americans across party lines, and it will often be hard to remember that it bears no resemblance to anything the Jewish Christian tradition has ever deemed orthodox. Nevertheless, it's standard procedure. And in a faithful reflection of these values, we insist that our presidents "step back from religion" while simultaneously giving lip service to everybody's own private, personal Jesus. Throughout much of American society, getting the job done, living in the real world (the business world), and being effective will demand the seemingly supernatural ability to step back from religion, and liberalism is a carefully designed attempt to overcome these conflicts of interests.

Religion, however, probably won't relinquish its prerogatives quite so easily. The kingdom of God won't settle for the title of "spiritual component" or a position as chaplain for a corporation or an ostensibly sovereign nation-state. It isn't content to serve as someone's "theological underpinnings" or "religious values." Like politics, it's a twenty-four-hour coverage, a battle for hearts, minds, and bodies, and the biblical witness announces that the Lord wants it all—the earth and everything in it, all authority. The Lord alone is sovereign. And the knowledge of the Lord will cover the earth as the waters cover the sea.

We are right to sense, within religious narratives, a movement larger than whatever manages to fit within our private pursuits of happiness, but this will always be the tension between a culture of life (never the property of any political party or magisterium) and the prerogatives of competing egos hell-bent on pursuing their narrowly defined self-interest. In a phrase that might have some connection with the life ethic we've recognized in the personalities of Lincoln and Presley, Joseph Cardinal Bernadin famously spoke of a seamless garment of life in his attempt to name a consistency of life ethic, a culture of pro-humanness that scandalizes our efforts to step away from faith or cast it aside long enough to return to the "real business" of private happiness accumulation. Our view of the grand scheme of our world needs to include more kinds of people and places than our narrower visions of success usually accommodate, and inheritors of the Jewish Christian tradition have always challenged themselves to expand their spheres of consideration to include the unwanted, the stranger, and the enemy. According to the biblical witness, there is an utterly unmarketable freedom, an unquantifiable goodness, and a wisdom that won't fit our sound bites, sales pitches, or conferrals of sovereignty. In American history, this culture has most often been associated, in some way, with people whose interpretation of the Bible challenged the status quo readings of their times, and its fruits are discernible in lending libraries, the abolitionist movement, advocates of women's suffrage, child labor laws, and the civil rights era. It is its own culture, not a phenomenon of private spirituality, and it will always sense a tension as it resides within various, never-completely-accommodating pagan cultures.

To be a learner of the larger freedom of a whole life ethic will require an unlearning of our habitual defensiveness and self-justification at all costs and an adoption of the easier yoke and lighter burden of confession. The coming kingdom does not respond well to the power of pride, it isn't subject to our privatizing impulse, and it is on the side of life and liberty in more ways than we can ask for or imagine. Confessing our inability to live faithfully to it might not always play well to onlookers near or far, but without this particular habit of speech, there is no life, liberty, or gospel.

And in His Own Mind He Shall Be Great

For those who are determined to live witness to the freedom of this coming kingdom in the rebellious here and now, examining the language with which we describe ourselves to ourselves and the way the words we hear will make us act, spend, and vote is a discipline we cannot afford to leave to strangers. When the forces behind media broadcasting primarily view citizens as target markets or potential voting demographics (soccer moms, NASCAR dads), avid consumers are drawn into a state of political dysfunction as ratings reach an all-time high. The fallout following the psychological warfare of a power grab is not conducive to the mental or emotional health of a community. And it's actually worse than that, because the power grab is unending, leaving no time for treatment or recovery or a moment to ask, in retrospect, "What was that all about?"

In a state of confused adoration toward clothing brands, celebrities, automobiles, sports figures, and the seekers (and holders) of public office, who have to buy their way onto the radar to be noticed, Americans are left trying to see and think clearly amid the static and the noise. According to the Jewish Christian tradition, we are already inclined to distort reality to suit our sense of self, and electronic media (in the hands of angry sinners, after all) will often accelerate this process. Largely cut off from redemptive participation in the life that surrounds us, we become less capable of perceiving in any effectual way our own moral deficiency, and Fred Friendly's worst-case scenarios are ever before us.

To my own mind, Friendly is an especially helpful guide, because I can't imagine him suggesting that destroying our televisions, radios, and Internet connections is the answer in curbing the contagion. He wouldn't mistake the technology for the content, but he would always ask if our media consumption is making us more or less capable of distinguishing between usable information and distracting nonissues that only serve to keep us glued and addicted. With this kind of methodology, we're able to think more rigorously as citizens and disciples and interact with an almost inevitably market-driven media whose stratagems, left to themselves, might make Gollums of us all.

When we let the terms "liberal" and "conservative" or "politics" and "religion" characterize an argument or a proposition before we've given ourselves the chance to consider them, we allow the unthinking shorthand well-suited for electronic media to infect our imaginations. To observe that it's a good thing that Jimmy Carter builds houses for poor people isn't an argument against any "conservative" position, and to be pleased to hear the news of the capture of Saddam Hussein isn't an argument in support of Republicans (or bad news for people who usually vote for Democrats). But it's becoming increasingly difficult for many Americans to consider history, information, or even everyday gossip apart from who appears momentarily to benefit the most from the disclosure. The self-deluding skill of judging all information in our own favor ("unbiased" if it's to our advantage; "biased" if it isn't) is a standard procedure for both sides of the split screen on our news networks, but it's also begun to contaminate our office space, our living rooms, and our houses of worship.

To apply Friendly's methodology a little differently, we might ask ourselves what we're trying to avoid thinking about when we reflexively say or think, "That's just your interpretation"; "This is only your opinion"; or "Timothy McVeigh/Osama Bin Laden/Saddam Hussein *is* absolute evil." What is it that we find reassuring in the assertion that terrorists think only about evil, "flat evil," and nothing else at any time? Who are we trying to convince? Simply thinking twice and looking hard for what our categories and knee-jerk responses conceal can become an especially effective form of exorcism. A twenty-four-hour fast from using the words "liberal," "conservative," "political," and "religious" might open whole new worlds.

To maintain that the first question for a Christian seeking political office should be whether or not the work can be pursued while simultaneously seeking first God's kingdom and righteousness is not a matter of "playing politics." And to assert, as a point of clarity, that equating America to "the light that shines in the darkness" is bad theology is not to twist matters to suit the Left or the Right. We have to remember that not all our observations fit neatly into a partisan slot. As we've noted, this is an incredibly difficult work in contemporary America, but our legacy of liberty is lost when we lose the ability to think past mischaracterizing categories and the will to ask questions to which we don't already know the answers. The tribal storytellers have to be engaged and challenged as they render us the service of trying to invent our reality for us. Being vigilant is not a matter of spending hours combing the Internet for jokes and stories that make our adversaries look stupid and our preferred parties righteous. Looking harder at their language and our own is the only way to sustain the interests of discipleship and democracy.

All Loveliness Is Anguish to Me

The anxious pressure we feel in our desire to hear (and then repeat to our families, friends, and coworkers) a sound-bite-worthy solution to what's wrong with the world or a masterful judgment that will put the paradox away is hostile to everything the biblical witness recognizes as wisdom. Jesus' admonition to "Judge not, lest ye be judged" and to call no person an idiot or a fool while carefully examining ourselves before attempting a word of discernment is binding upon our media consumption. Fred Friendly anticipated the power of media either to model the virtues of delayed judgment in the direction of better social practice or to incite minds toward defensive, endlessly self-justifying postures. Although the open hand is clearly more representative of biblical insight than the clenched fist, both express the natural desire to keep chaos at bay. But the former recognizes the possibility of madness and crimes against humanity within oneself while the latter rejects, with passionate intensity, the suggestion that we might have a log or two in our own eyes.

The other half of that teaching that is often forgotten is the idea that *seeing clearly* is the goal: "Then you will see clearly to take the speck out of your neighbor's eye" (Luke 6:39–42). And the goal is a means to the end of actually being a help to one's neighbor. But no clear vision is possible for those who boast of (or worse, really believe in) their own logless vision, a vision of no spin. And those who, in their desire to battle the forces of chaos (right/left-wing conspiracies or evildoers always *out there*), deem themselves worthy of the ring of great power (think of Tolkien's Boromir, Denethor, Saruman, and Gollum) will find themselves governed by a persistent illusion. We might also recall the folk wisdom offered in Beck's observation that death has a way of creeping in slowly till we feel safe in its arms. Boiling point is only approached in not-quite-discernible stages, and the frog in the beaker won't know what's happening until it's too late.

While the devil is probably too much the devil ever to make a straightforward deal with any of his supposed business partners, and no evildoers in history ever self-consciously or publicly recognize themselves as such while fighting to put down other evildoers, literature will often afford us language whereby violent souls actually talk about what they're doing while they're doing it. I allude to Tolkien in an effort to urge a more critical eye in the direction of our endlessly self-justifying tendencies (what the church sometimes refers to as the doctrine of original sin), and as Shakespeare always seems to offer an illuminating word for any and all issues that beset us, we now turn to a deeply troubled Macbeth. With his wife's help, he's already talked himself into murdering his king and the one friend who dared to question his career ambitions. Like most media consumers, he's now looking for a destiny forecast (the witches whose broadcast set him down this path in the first place will do). Wondering how he might best capitalize on events to make sure everything's going his way, he offers the following on how he might best go for the gold:

> For mine own good,
> All causes shall give way: I am in blood
> Stepp'd in so far that, should I wade no more,
> Returning were as tedious as go o'er:
> Strange things I have in head, that will to hand;
> Which must be acted ere they may be scann'd.[5]

While actors, politicians, musicians, and athletes might say this kind of thing in an especially candid discussion of career goals with their managers, this brand of bluster won't be spoken aloud except in sleep, under hypnosis, and by characters in Shakespeare's plays. As an English teacher, I'm always trying to apply the words of regicides and other poor players to something a little closer to home. And for an American thinking through personal finances, values, what becomes of taxpayers' money, and what to make of current events, there are some lines here that might strike a chord.

With no vision beyond the inner logic of improvised explanations, Macbeth proclaims, "For mine own good, / All causes shall give way."[6] We're human; therefore we angle and improvise, but if the first thought in our minds when we hear news is, "Does this make my group look good or bad?" or "How does this reflect on my self-image?" then something might be going awry in our ability to see clearly. What we anxiously perceive as gospel for our own individualistic fortunes is often bad news for friends, family, and foreign nations. Macbeth's dismissal of the possibility of regret or repentance (it's too tedious to step back through the blood he's left on the tracks) bears a disturbing resemblance to the false strength of "No Regrets, No Mistakes, No Admission of Fallible Vision Even in Retrospect" that is an everpresent temptation within American culture. The pretense of omnipotence might play well in prime time, but it flies in the face of all received wisdom from the Bible to Shakespeare to Tolkien.

For a more precise word of challenge (an American one) against the darker impulses of an often-unacknowledged American mythology, we have an American prophet in Herman Melville. Borrowing heavily from the Bible and Shakespeare, Melville expresses ongoing skepticism concerning the absolute trustworthiness of human hearts (Emersonian or otherwise) and seems to think that this might be where the uniquely American trouble starts. The crew of the *Pequod* are beginning to realize that their captain, Ahab, is tragically fixated on gaining vengeance over an animal blissfully unaware of Ahab's existence. When I listen to a friend, neighbor, or family member rant against a president (say a Bush or a Clinton), whom they've never met and with whom they will never exchange a word, and the tone and demeanor of the talk takes a turn for the apoplectic, I want to adapt Starbuck's words to whale-mad Ahab and cry, "Madness! To be enraged with a face on television seems blasphemous. What profit will thy anger yield thee? Go have a cup of coffee with thy wife or telephone thy child or dine ye with a homeless person."[7] But the pervading excitement of media addiction is often such that the addict will tolerate no companions except on condition of their perfect sympathy with the addict's present state of feeling. I should add that Starbuck's words come to me self-administered. The allure of issue-driven newspeak has an alarming way of distracting me from the more needful and local concerns that could do with my attention. All too often, the siren song of electronic soul molesters (Baptist minister Will Campbell's term) draws me away from the company of actual living people.

But what makes Starbuck's rebuke especially tragic is that he hasn't told Ahab anything Ahab doesn't know. Like Macbeth, Ahab is a diligent student of his own downward spiral, and, like many Americans, he knows all is not well in his angry and weary soul. "All loveliness is anguish to me,"[8] he confesses, because, like Milton's Satan, he is damned most subtly and malignantly in the midst of Paradise. And like Gollum, he can only read the world though the lens of his own covetousness: "I'm demoniac, I am madness maddened! That wild madness that's only calm to comprehend itself!"[9] If anyone feels compelled to accept my advice concerning a twenty-four-hour fast from the highly charged, hot-button words (liberal, conservative, bias, agenda) that keep us from thinking clearly, I'd also like to recommend (alongside Old and New Testament readings) chapter 37 of *Moby Dick,* from which these phrases are drawn. Ahab feels his brain beating against what seems like the solid metal of a steel skull and imagines the path of his fixed purpose to be laid with iron rails, whereon his soul is grooved to run. Some time before the Internet, William Gibson, and the near omnipresent sensory assault of multinational corporations, looking to sell and outsource, Melville penned this soliloquy concerning an iron necessity of self-seeking soul destruction, but I suspect there's a timeliness to it that strikes closer to our national psyche than we'd like to admit: "Over unsounded gorges, through the rifled hearts of mountains, under torrents' beds, unerringly I rush! Naught's an obstacle, naught's an angle to the iron way!"[10]

I Contain Multitudes

Starting from weirded-out Nashville, where I was born, I was taught (like Ahab, Starbuck, and perhaps every American president) to view myself in some sense as an eternal soul. Haunted by the thought of what this might mean and alarmed at how cavalier most of my comrades were on the subject of eternity, I mostly associated this preoccupation with church services and that black Bible I figured I'd better read all the way through before it was too late. I don't regret my early childhood preoccupation with eternity in any way, but I know I was often tempted to view any and all life that didn't line up with my thoughts of eternity as tragically irrelevant to everything that really mattered, because all that mattered (wasn't it obvious?) was eternity.

To the extent that I began to view my passion for eternity as somehow nearer to the appropriate level of intensity than the passion levels of my peers, I suppose I fit the description of what is often termed a fundamentalist. But I don't think this habit of mind and imagination is limited to those who consider themselves religious, since demonizing the opposition appears to be a universal inclination. To my thinking, it was with the presumed backing of the eternal that I passed reluctant judgment on all the interesting worldly things that, as far as I could tell, had no inheritance in the infinite. My enjoyment of the not eternally significant day-to-day was made only a little bit guilty by my suspicion that it was all going to burn. I had yet to view the Lord's Prayer as a calling of God's kingdom "on earth," and I probably viewed heaven as a little more like a netherworld or a phantom zone. This odd doctrine of unincarnate faith (mostly constructed in my own mind) began to be challenged in a high school English class when I turned in my literature book to a section called "Transcendentalism" and thought, "That's more like it."

What a word: *Transcendentalist*. And what a thing to be. The whole thing seemed remarkably and scandalously grounded. Could I really have it both ways? Heaven *and* earth? Walt Whitman seemed to think so: "The SOUL: Forever and forever—longer than soil is brown and solid—longer than water ebbs and flows."[11] And even better: "I say the whole earth, and all the stars in the sky, are for Religion's sake."[12] Here was a poetry of new potentialities and an affirmation of what I'd begun to glimpse in the paintings of Howard Finster, what I'd already seen in particular episodes of *The Twilight Zone*, and what I thought I was hearing in the music of Lone Justice and R.E.M., a uniquely American mysticism I was tempted to call country music—comprehensive and curious but confident at nobody's expense. What does this have to do with the national psyche?

For one thing, it points in the direction of an alternative to the death-dealing dichotomies that drive so much best-selling, most-viewed deliberation on America, the rest of the world, and the future; an alternative to the Ahab curse that hastens America's nervous breakdown. Just as Allen Ginsberg's "Howl" will insist that all things human are somehow scandalously holy, Whitman submits, as a to-be-agreed-on basis for all speech and conversation and politics, the creed that all matter is charged with the grandeur of God; that the spiritual resides within all material (no nonspiritual, secular, or nonsouled human beings). We won't see clearly until we look humbly: "Bring all the art and science of the world, and baffle and humble it with one spear of grass." As Macbeth and Ahab look upon creation, they feel mocked and anxious that life won't deliver on their mad desires or that they'll lose the ground they've insanely concluded is their own and no one else's. The affection that should have gone into treasuring the life around us, the people nearby, gets drained by our contempt for whoever's on the wrong side of our issues. The beauty and complexity of the created world becomes irrelevant to our fixations. Against the blind and unreasoning rush, Whitman describes a single blade of grass as the journey-work of the stars.

I can hardly think of Whitman's insistent hopefulness without imagining the witness of Studs Terkel, whose hope for America (like Whitman's) always includes the notion of outgoing love as a moral imperative. Specifically, I recall a moment on television when Terkel was shown a copy of Nick Ut's 1972 Pulitzer Prize-winning photo of a nine-year-old Kim Phuc, naked and on fire, fleeing a napalm attack. When asked what the image brought to his mind, Terkel quickly responded that this is our child, everybody's child, a moment of anguish for all people, an occasion for grief and urgent communal embrace. Our child. Not someone else's. Ours. Us. Terkel casually makes an appeal to the conservatively communal sensibility that insists on a reverencing of children; the ancient folk wisdom that says you should never walk past or look upon a child without speaking a word of blessing. And with an unmistakable degree of authority as an experienced connoisseur of American culture, Terkel seemed to suggest that the meaning of America resides in our ability to say, without qualification, "Our child."

For many Americans, life is so full of persecution complex, fears of being tricked or made to feel guilty, and anxious anticipation of spin that we've come close to losing our ability to listen and look without defensiveness. We risk becoming unable to look at or speak to the world without assuming an adversarial posture, so in love with our abstractions that we can't look at human beings properly.We can hardly think of suffering children without feeling manipulated by an interest group. It doesn't have to be this way. And if we're going to engage the world without losing our souls, we won't let it be. Or as Sly and the Family Stone remind us, we're going to have to adjust our sense of self and untopple the tyranny of mad individualism, because we have to live together. We don't have to hold ourselves aloof from the troubled everybody who people our everyday. We *are* they. We're everyday people, and everybody is a star.

Long after discovering Whitman as a high schooler, it was pointed out to me that the Lord's Prayer isn't a call to be transported from the wicked world into unearthly, disembodied bliss, but a call for God's abundance, God's shalom. It is a call to be fully manifested *on earth* as it already is in the heavens, a cry for regime change within a rebellious world that does not acknowledge its Maker in the way it treats people or regards itself. And all language, whether broadcast by entertainment conglomerates, news networks, or radio talk-show hosts and their avid listeners, is unavoidably, if unconsciously, theological. We can't speak of people or politics without speaking of the eternal. I began to remember what Martin Luther King Jr. and Dorothy Day never forgot: It's all religion whether we like it or not. In Whitman's invocation of American ensemble (always looking to bring in all nations, "I'd sow a seed for thee of endless nationality"), a note of eschatological hope resonates with both Gandhi's confidence in satyagraha and C. S. Lewis's description of great divorce:

I have no mockings or arguments, I witness and wait.

"Song of Myself"

Roaming in thought over the Universe, I saw the little that is Good
    steadily hastening towards immortality,
And the vast all that is call'd Evil I saw hastening to merge itself
    and become lost and dead.

"Roaming in Thought"

As the American creed of liberty and justice for all humanity takes on new and unexpected forms beyond the limitations of whatever we've settled for in the way of unequal justice and license mistaken for liberty, a vigilance against our Ahab-like mind-sets will be crucial. Religion is practice. Politics is practice. Religion is politics is what we do and how we speak and the way we think about other human beings. And America's cultural heritage is blessedly fraught with voices that won't let us forget it. Whitman's musings and Terkel's casual remark concerning the image of a child that many Americans once imagined to be an enemy of freedom are touchstones. They can reactivate our moral imagination against our darker trends of world-is-vampire, midnight vultures, and big-fish-eat-little-one, which often portray themselves as homeland security issues, free trade, and, tragically, the American way. Fred Friendly believed there was more room for more rich conversation than we've begun to guess, and the wise voices within our national life have more to say. The voices bear ample witness against the myopic moralism that falls so short of our more comprehensive, compassionate best. Do we have the ears to hear? Do we want to?

Chapter 3

No Celestial Railroads:
A Literature for Democracy

But all the things that God would have us do are hard for us to do—remember that—and hence, he oftener commands us than endeavors to persuade. And if we obey God, we must disobey ourselves; and it is in this disobeying ourselves, wherein the hardness of obeying God consists.
—Herman Melville, Moby Dick

I wish God had given me the faculty of writing a sunshiny book.
—*Nathaniel Hawthorne, letter to James T. Fields*

Good God, I can't publish this. We'd both be in jail.
—*William Faulkner's account of his publisher's response to his work*

Oh a State begins to take form in the stateless German night, a state that spans oceans and surface politics, sovereign as the International or the Church of Rome, and the Rocket is its soul.
Thomas Pynchon, Gravity's Rainbow

*O*n the subject of the new day dawning all around him, Ralph Waldo Emerson noted the presence of something strange in the neighborhood when he observed, "It is said to be the age of the first person singular." The "Our Father" would become "My Father"; a turn inward was becoming possible for more and more people; and a very different kind of doctrine (political? religious?) was gaining ground, what

Emerson called "the infinitude of the private man." Emerson didn't invent American individualism any more than Martin Luther founded the notion of church reform. But just as Luther expressed regret over how calling into question the teachings of one particular pope sent shockwaves that left many a man on many a dung hill in Germany fancying himself his own pope, I can imagine Emerson scratching his head over many a postmodern notion of self-reliance, the health hazards of sitting in front of a television trying to believe in yourself, and the trite language with which many Americans attempt to explain their moral deficiencies: "I'm so sorry *you feel that way,*" "I regret *that you misunderstood me,*" "I apologize *if you were offended,*" and "I'm sorry that *people seeing those pictures didn't understand* the true nature and heart of America."

Strange days when requests for forgiveness are substituted with statements of regret over wrong impressions. I think of the mogul of all matter on *The Simpsons,* Montgomery C. Burns, and his determination to own all media outlets for the sake of self-image: "Well I'm going to change this town's accurate impression of me." If all we really regret is someone's ability to deduce who we are, is there any soul left to forfeit?

The language of confession, of actually repenting of one's sins of spin and self-love, is replaced by the strange concept of expressing regret that someone failed in his or her attempt to understand your true nature, your true heart, and how your words and actions bear no relation to your pristine, true, only-selfless-intentioned and pure self. Sorry about that (and only that). Admittedly, Emerson didn't create Sheilaism, Jerry Springer (the phenomenon, not the man), or a news media that recognizes the above instances of self-abusing language as "formal apologies." I bring Emerson into the proceedings only to suggest that these trends have been with us for some time and that the madness of the moment has been prepared for. You can resist Emerson's belief that the sincere and simple man who worships God somehow becomes God (the tyranny of sincerity?) without losing the better notion that all people, though occasionally suffering a delusion or two, bear God-given dignity. In F. O. Matthiessen's magisterial study *American Renaissance,* we're told that Emerson, Hawthorne, Thoreau, Whitman, and Melville self-consciously composed literature *for* democracy and hoped to help build "a culture commensurate with America's political opportunity."[1] This chapter will focus on Hawthorne and Melville while also locating, along this continuum, William Faulkner and Thomas Pynchon. I propose that their visions (on the local, national, and international levels) serve to curb the danger among the peoples of the Earth (Americans not excepted) to idolize themselves into states of imbecility. I take it that this is what redemptive visions are for.

Matthiessen wanted his readers to "feel the challenge of our still undiminished resources,"[2] a literature that would equip democratic culture against the clear and present danger of a culture of deception. And while I can't very well beam into the back of anyone's head (*Matrix*-style) what I take to be the mostly untapped wisdom of these figures, I will try to explain why these writers might serve as a sanity-restoring, soul-saving supplement to the average American's media diet; some forgotten transmissions that might tell better stories of adultery, severe domestic dysfunction, and demon possession than what we've grown accustomed to calling entertainment. The works that marketeers classify as "literary classics" are sometimes a harder pill than popular music, movies, and science fiction, but all we can do is try. We need media that will help our words (*freedom, love, terror, mercy, evil, forgiveness, democracy*) regain their heft. When they lose their heft, we're tools for whatever contagion best suits the stratagems of the prospering wicked. We lose the ability to question someone else's abstractions, and we're left with little means to learn or understand better stories than whatever seems to suit our anxious projections of ourselves. The cultural legacy is there if we're looking hard enough. And it is there in spades.

Unclose Your Eyes

As a master of the warping thought, Nathaniel Hawthorne creates the impression that he would worry less if he thought we were worrying enough over what we make of ourselves and others in our teeming brains. Like the other authors under examination, he forged an American literature that treads firmly on the ground, but his stories did so by painting the pictures we create and mistake for realities. His characters have a difficult time reaching past their images of each other to communicate or achieve anything in the way of intimacy. They have to remind themselves that life is infinitely larger than all their well-meant formulations and tightly held suspicions, and the same goes for other lives. They're all spooked, one way or another, and it seems clear that Hawthorne told these stories in an effort to, in some fashion, unspook himself. There is a quiet selfishness that can easily become a habit of mind (to be resisted daily) and, in turn, a morbid vanity that makes of our reflexive thinking, to borrow a military term, an antipersonnel weapon. This breed of emotional disorder will make inhumane behavior and imaginings feel like dire necessity. As is the case for many American writers, getting this process down on paper appears to be one way Hawthorne devised of raging against the dying of the light.

In *Twice-Told Tales*, Hawthorne manages to prognosticate in the direction of the mad mind-set (Macbeth, Ahab, news junkie) discussed in the previous chapter. In a strange meditation called "The Haunted Mind," he describes the sensation of being "wide awake in a realm of illusions . . . an intermediate space, where the business of life does not intrude."[3] And in an odd premonition of the sensation of television viewing (or the memory of television), he imagines a state in which "the mind has a passive sensibility, but no active strength: when the imagination is a mirror, imparting vividness to all ideas, without the power of selecting or controlling them."[4] The mind is left with no active strength to select, control, or properly discern the increasingly vivid ideas that come to it. And as "things of the mind become dim spectres to the eye,"[5] we're left to search desperately for whatever might remind us of the living world and whatever stories we used to inhabit that made life meaningful.

Most maddening of all, we will tend to mistake these dim spectres for heartfelt visions and our heartfelt visions for weighty truths. This is where Hawthorne offers both a reforming word to the less admirable habits of thought among his Puritan forebears and a corrective to the Emersonian mind's way of confusing blissed-out moments of emotional intensity for stairways to heaven. When we say, "God," "Truth," "Righteousness," "Eternity," or "Liberty," we'd better have a voice near at hand whispering, "You don't know quite what you're talking about." Otherwise, we burn witches, persecute the most righteous in the name of righteousness, or justify various modes of death-dealing selfishness in the name of personal self-fulfillment. Discerning between tough, not-to-be-mastered, eternal reality and our momentary, multiplying illusions will involve no easy shortcuts, no matter how powerfully we feel them in our well-meaning hearts.

In what was conceived as an updated addendum to Bunyan's *Pilgrim's Progress,* Hawthorne envisioned a visit to the city of Destruction in "The Celestial Railroad." While touring the area, he decides to indulge a curiosity concerning what is purported to be a direct railway line to the Celestial City. After boarding the train, Hawthorne meets a character named Mr. Smooth-it-away, a native townsman of Destruction, who happens to be the railroad's visionary director and one of its largest stockholders in this enterprise of streamlined spirituality. At a station house erected over the narrow Wicket-gate of Bunyan's story, tickets to the Celestial City are dispensed, and Hawthorne declines to offer an opinion as to whether they will be as readily received at the gate as Bunyan's antique rolls of parchment, though he notes that they're certainly more conveniently carried. While Prince Beelzebub once shot deadly arrows at earnest pilgrims approaching the narrow gate, "the enlightened Directors of the railroad" have now worked out a mutual compromise, having employed the Prince's minions at the station house. Needless to say, the Celestial Railroad is a farce, as the genuine, better-grounded pilgrims of Vanity Fair inform him, and the better-selling spirituality of Smooth-it-away will end with a fatal ferry-boat ride in a water whose deadly chill will never leave, "until Death be drowned in his own river." The narrator wakes from his dream.

As we can see, Hawthorne shared with Melville a contempt for easy abstractions (whether extolled by transcendentalists or the self-proclaimed gatekeepers of sound religious teaching). Words had to put on flesh. In a letter to Hawthorne, Melville remarked, "As soon as you say Me, a God, a Nature, so soon you jump off from your stool and hang from the beam. Yes, that word is the hangman. Take God out of the dictionary, and you would have Him in the street."[6]

Wisdom will involve knowing that our signifiers do not equal the eternal absolute, and holding on to the blessed dirty and watery earth (amid the images, slogans, and dim spectres) will require the ongoing recognition that we're strangely drawn to easy untruth much of the time. The danger of taking one's blind, religious fervor for divine illumination was inextricably bound to the ancestry of these men, and faithfulness would require moving forward, praying for improved DNA. In a letter to Melville, Hawthorne writes, "Let us thank God for having given us such ancestors; and let each successive generation thank Him, not less fervently, for being one step further from them in the march of ages."[7]

We should note the remarkably progressive understanding of history and human grasp of the divine as Hawthorne expresses the hope that future generations will thank God for their distance from the grim delusions of his own. Like Dostoevsky and Flannery O'Connor, Hawthorne and Melville were troubled by haunted minds that deemed themselves unhaunted and by the belief that truth was straightforward, simple, and easily accessible to all good and decent people, available for any reasoning person's assent in an unembodied, unincarnate, sphere of theological theory (Puritan *or* transcendentalist). As students of the Bible, Hawthorne and Melville understood that goodness and decency are stranger matters than most admit, and a culture *of* the people, *for* the people, and *by* the people would require looking at people and their actions as more paradoxical than grandiloquent generalizations and deadly abstractions allow. Telling it like it is and not how our vanity would like it to be (what Melville called "the usable truth") can open eyes to God in the street, the neighbor next door, and the never-uninteresting everybody. We're all fallen *and* redeemed, and fiction can tease us back into this tension. Melville observed, "It is with fiction as with religion; it should present another world, and yet one to which we feel the tie."[8] Understanding and trying to do good within one's present will be to partake in a muddy mystery. Fiction reminds us that we don't know what we're doing. In an echo of Lincoln's thoughts on God's will and human passions, Hawthorne noted, "His instruments have no consciousness of His purpose; if they imagine they have, it is a pretty sure token they are *not* His instruments."[9]

Let the Black Flower Blossom

Hawthorne's world is awash in histories, resentments, misunderstandings, obsessions, and hopes through (and in spite of) which God is somehow accomplishing redemption. This is the atmosphere of phantasmagoric forms in which Hawthorne's characters live out their existence. He understands that disengaging ourselves from our worst imaginings—the theater of envy that makes real truthfulness, genuine generosity, and actual community next to impossible—will be a journey down a narrow path. Hawthorne worked in the days before mass media and the broadband that leads to destruction. But it might be appropriate to apply the wisdom of Hawthorne's tale of adultery and unforgiveness, *The Scarlet Letter,* to our own strange days.

The ideas that fester within wronged husband Roger Chillingworth aren't exactly thoughts or arguments, but they are definitely passions, and his raging, vengeful pride can possess him utterly while also, Hawthorne wryly notes, passing for a kind of calmness. He can be filled top to toe with direst cruelty, with writhing horror twisting across his features, dead without knowing it, but remarkably in control. His smiles of "dark and self-relying intelligence"[10] will come off as the most professional, upright expressions of a man in possession of himself while Hester Prynne, his estranged, legal wife, will see in him a man committed to the formal ruin, consecutive and slow, of his own soul.

Somehow, as the possessor of that ignominious brand, the scarlet "A," Hester has developed a talent, not for seeing dead people, but for feeling the glance of every self-deceived, downward-spiral-bound, closet degenerate in view, namely, everyone around her at one time or another. She is blessed or cursed with a strange sympathy, because if truth were made fully known, the scarlet letter would blaze on many a bosom. Freed from the perfunctory practice of putting on the appearance of righteousness, Hester can see and feel everything, and, for all of her suffering, it is the most awful and loathsome aspect of her existence. When in the company of the community's moral pillars, whom her society views as "mortal man in fellowship with angels,"[11] Hester is moved to ask herself, "What evil thing is at hand?"[12] Against the airtight mythology of respectability and moral superiority that often seizes self-identified religious communities, Hawthorne's vision of a pre-1776 America is a jeremiad, within which Hester sees in every face a sociopath. But unlike Hawthorne's Young Goodman Brown, for whom all humans in view will now undergo a witch trial in his deranged head (contemporary popular discourse in America?), Hester will work tremblingly toward moral enlightenment and a vocation as an especially sympathetic Sister of Mercy: "This badge hath taught me,—it daily teaches me,—it is teaching me at this moment."[13] She's come to understand that nobody is in a position to cast the first stone, and she's liberated by the insight.

Like many a preacher, priest, or politician whose livelihood involves portraying oneself as a professional good and decent person, Arthur Dimmesdale, the secret father of Hester's child, longs to cry out to his parishioners, "I, your pastor, whom you so reverence and trust, am utterly a pollution and a lie!"[14] But apart from the obligatory "humble, unworthy sinner" talk of a modest man (what Hawthorne calls "a remorseful hypocrite") and his standing on the scaffold in the middle of the night, hands joined with Hester and their child, Pearl, Dimmesdale's role as "a professional teacher of truth" repeatedly compels him to defer a public focus on his family till Judgment Day. Noting his unwillingness to live up to his convictions, Pearl laughs at him, informing him (as if his troubled soul needed reminding) that he is neither bold nor true.

Although Dimmesdale is not shown waiting (via video camera) while Maury Povich opens an envelope to reveal Pearl's lineage to a studio audience as Hester weeps and Chillingworth rages, we have here a troubled scenario that we couldn't call too terribly uncommon to our day or Hawthorne's. But keeping the imagination sane in these dismal mazes requires a wisdom not afforded by viewers calling in ("You decide! We want to hear from you!") or someone getting voted off an island. The role of the accuser (like the seat of judgment) is not suited for mental or emotional stability. Hawthorne says of Chillingsworth, "A striking evidence of man's faculty of transforming himself into a devil, if he will only, for a reasonable space of time, undertake a devil's office"[15] (Viewers and listeners repent!).

There is a mode of internal dialogue that will play like a broken loop till we own up to ourselves and others. Dimmesdale's thought life is a "constant introspection wherewith he tortured, but could not purify himself."[16] But Hester Prynne is submitted as an apostle of coming revelation (fit for democracy) bearing witness within a hostile, uncomprehending, bewitched community. A moral that saves but won't necessarily play well on camera or boost approval ratings: "Be true! Be true! Be true! Show freely to the world, if not your worst, yet some trait whereby the worst may be inferred."[17] Timely words for a culture with the occasional puritanical tendency, a sense of Manifest Destiny, and an unfortunate habit of rewriting history to suits its sense of moral superiority. *The Scarlet Letter* admonishes us toward a costly vigilance required for any political, religious community that wants to avoid destroying itself from within. Hawthorne reminds us that telling the truth (and thereby shaming the devil) might be the first step in any war on terror.

That Multiple Pilgrim Species, Man

In his praise of Hawthorne (to whom he dedicated *Moby Dick*), Melville counted him among "those writers who breathe that unshackled, democratic spirit of Christianity in all things."[18] Returning for a moment to the imagery of timelines and continuums, I can't help but think of Melville as the figure who most forcefully brings the imaginations of Shakespeare and William Blake to bear on the Declaration of Independence, claiming them on behalf of his understanding of liberty for all. Melville assumes that Christianity, properly understood, is unfailingly pro-human. Dissecting human freedom how he may, Melville knows he only goes skin deep, and the awe he feels toward his predecessors' ways with words only invigorates further his sense of the possibilities of freer and truer expression: "All that has been said but multiplies the avenues to what remains to be said."[19]

Just as Hawthorne ran counter to the dominant, self-described religious impulses of his age by making an adultress the voice of prophetic witness, Melville takes boundless sympathy toward all human forms to be a biblical (and democratic) imperative. Beginning *Moby Dick* by way of a bold self-identification with one whom many in the West would presume to be eternally cast off from the covenant ("Call me Ishmael"), our narrator begins with a more magnanimous eye than his readers would be prepared for. He is called to see God's image in the face of the tattooed cannibal, the meanest of mariners and castaways, and whatever passes for "the least of these." The goodness of God toward his rebellious children founds democracy by decreeing God's image in any and every human dress:

> This august divinity I treat of, is not the dignity of kings and robes, but that abounding dignity which has no robed investiture. Thou shalt see it shining in the arm that wields a pick or drives a spike; that democratic dignity which, on all hands, radiates without end from God; Himself! the great God absolute! The centre and circumference of all democracy! His omnipresence, our divine equality.[20]

God illumined "the swart convict, Bunyan"[21] and lifted "the stumped and paupered arm of Cervantes,"[22] and now Melville (call him Ishmael) prays that tragic grace will surround his sympathetic portrayals of his disreputable cast: "Bear me out in it, thou great democratic God!"[23] As John Milton invoked the heavenly muse that once inspired Moses to show him how to justify the ways of God to men, Ishmael wants to make the world safer for democracy by witnessing God's comprehensive purposes (more mysterious than we can know) as he explores strange new worlds and seeks out new life forms and new civilizations. The unknown is neither strange nor new for Melville's democratic God ("the magnanimous God of heaven and earth—pagans and all included"[24]), and if this is so, perhaps we need not be so squeamish or xenophobic nor so quick to assume ourselves somehow already sufficiently converted to the ways of the Almighty. Perhaps the dignity that radiates without end from God extends further than we've begun to guess.

With an everlasting itch for things remote and the belief that "ignorance is the parent of fear,"[25] Ishmael dismisses as most demonic of all the fastidiousness that would make of the stranger a demon and the cry of "Heathen!" as a devilish obstruction to neighbor love. Concerning the cannibal Queequeg he says, "The man's a human being just as I am: he has just as much reason to fear me, as I have to be afraid of him."[26] What a profoundly democratic sensibility. Gold, heredity, nationalism, and pride of place are the instrumentalities Hawthorne would refer to as "the big, heavy, solid unrealities"[27] that keep us from thinking properly of one another as children of God and aspiring Americans. These are idols to which Ishmael will not bow down. And between Queequeg and Ahab we can note myriad ways that one can go about worshiping that which, by nature, is not a god. As a sailor, Ishmael will dutifully follow his orders but with a mind toward a great reversal that, now and later, can put present anxieties in perspective: "What does that indignity amount to, I mean, in the scales of the New Testament?"[28] He trusts that bosses won't be bosses forever. And given the biblical word on the last and the first and the manner in which the unrealities jerk a person about like a mixed-up marionette, Ishmael rhetorically asks, "Who ain't a slave?"[29]

The questions of freedom, savagery, civilization, authority, and reading reality rightly haunt Ishmael at every turn. Ahab moves his arm up and down and wonders aloud if it is he or omnipotent God who wills it. And in another Lincolnian turn, Ishmael hears a sermon before the voyage begins as a certain Father Mapple expounds upon the story of Jonah with the qualifier "I have read ye by what murky light may be mine,"[30] as he calls upon his congregation to stand against "the proud gods and commodores of the earth."[31] Warned against the idolatries that delude human thinking, Ishmael begins to have notions that would scandalize the commonplaces of his day when, for instance, he looks upon the face of a sleeping Queequeg and is oddly reminded of the popular busts of George Washington's head. Ishmael assures us that he was raised as a normal, self-respecting Presbyterian, but his constructs are slightly undone by the likes of Queequeg, who seems to possess "a nature in which there lurked no civilized hypocrisies and bland deceits."[32] Daring to sense God's affection for an infidel who suddenly strikes him as somehow quintessentially American, he feels as if a burning coal has made new his unclean lips: "I felt a melting in me. No more my splintered heart and maddened hand were turned against the wolfish world. This soothing savage had redeemed it."[33]

At the risk of digression, somewhere between Ishmael's renunciation of the fearful ignorance of racism and Studs Terkel's affirmation of "Our child," I'd like to recall a moment on fifties-era

American television when Steve Allen asked Jack Kerouac, something of a spokesman for the Beat Generation, for a definition of the term "Beat." Almost before he'd finished the question, Kerouac responded, "Sympathetic." The posture of the Beat moment is one of mutual beatenness before the world, and to feel worn down, tempted toward melancholy but not despairing, is to be heartbroken in the direction of increased sympathy for all creation groaning and awaiting redemption. And if the alternative to this brand of beatitude is unsympathetic posture, uncompassionate and not prone to solidarity, then the venom with which a Kerouac says a word like "Square" seems pretty well justified. Right up there with "hypocrites," "blind guides," "racist," "fascist," and "brood of vipers." Ishmael looks upon Queequeg and is seized by the revelation that he's just like everyone else. Ishmael speaks forth an acknowledgment of democratic dignity, perceiving an individual conscience equal to his own. Really believing it, as Lincoln understood, is to come upon a stumbling block to the tyranny of our maddened hands. The clichéd quality of the insight risks becoming so commonplace that we lose the sense of the costly moral epiphany it was and is to suggest such a thing. They're like us. From Queequeg to Vietnam to Baghdad, do we see ourselves in these images? Does it slow us down? Is our royal "We" larger than our political party or our national borders? Do we sense solidarity out there? Do we really want democratic revolution, or are we preparing to pull up the drawbridge? Are we squares or are we Americans?

Ishmael is quick to recognize his own "maddened hand" assuming a destructively adversarial posture in "the wolfish world." There is a distempered spirit, easily discerned in Ahab and in much so-called political debate in our own day, that can only speak in conversation-stoppers while resenting news that might require a slower, more measured response than the quick sound bite or easy putdown of the newsbearer's "agenda." The mind so possessed will not see, because it does not feel. This is the opposite of the disposition (Beat, sympathetic, slow to judgment) that Ishmael assumes in the telling of his story. He'd prayed that God would bear him out in his storytelling concerning the august divinity of humankind, and in *Moby Dick,* Ishmael's unprecedentedly American and radically magnanimous voice would gain an audience and gradual vindication as it played progenitor to various humane sensibilities we now take for granted. We still haven't gotten to the bottom of it.

Alike in Ignorance

What will not do, for this tradition of American truth telling under the gaze of a God who radiates dignity without end, is to hold oneself aloof from the only-seeing-in-part communion of the all-having-sinned-and-fallen-short sainthood. This is not a problem for Ishmael. He looks at people (from Queequeg to Ahab) and creation itself as not-to-be-conquered mysteries, and he has no problem with the we-only-know-in-part part of the biblical witness. In continuity with Lincoln, Hawthorne, Martin Luther King Jr., the Beats, and *The Simpsons*, he proclaims, "Heaven have mercy on us all—Presbyterians and Pagans alike—for we are all somehow dreadfully cracked about the head, and sadly need mending."[34] His is a most comprehensive soul, and when Captain Bildad (part owner of the *Pequod* with Captain Peleg) seems inclined to deny Queequeg employment on account of his failure to be a member of a Christian church, Ishmael explains that, on the contrary, Queequeg's a practicing member of the First Congregational Church. What church is this? Ishmael explains:

> I mean, sir, the same ancient Catholic Church to which you and I, and Captain Peleg there, and Queequeg here, and all of us, and every mother's son and soul of us belong; the great and everlasting First Congregation of this whole worshipping world; we all belong to that; only some of us cherish some queer crotchets noways touching the grand belief; in *that* we all join hands.[35]

Bildad catches his drift: "I never heard a better sermon." We all worship in one way or another (as the apostle Paul observed in conversation with the Athenians in Acts), and in our efforts to worship well, we all hold a screwy doctrine or two that will burn away like chaff when the real thing comes. In this variously dissembling silliness we can all join hands in strict solidarity, a creed worthy of Waffle

House fellowship, a "Heaven have mercy on us all" that could color all our speech.

Ishmael's improvised justification for a more hospitable reception for the outsider is characteristic of the vocation Melville will ply for the sake of a healthier democracy and a less self-deluding Christianity. Ishmael's speech is frank and free and exemplary as an idiom counter to the Ahab-like megalomania that loudly offers itself from time to time as the real America, tarnishing our better broadcasts throughout history. We need the idiom like we need a more tragic orientation in our talk of truth and victory and guarantees; an idiom better suited to a patchwork nation built by immigrant hands and founded on immigration—a nation at its best when pressing forward to better ways of being human in a land of and for the free.

Alike in ignorance, whether thinking too little or too much, the humanity aboard the *Pequod* exhibits the dark wisdom and rude brilliance that Ishmael sees in every human face. But the biblical witness that mocks any and all supposed human grandeur profoundly informs Ishmael's study of man and beast: "There is no folly of the beasts of the earth which is not infinitely outdone by the madness of men."[36] A troubled and conscientious awareness of human folly is a prerequisite for truthful speech and sane imaginings, and in this regard, Jesus, the Man of Sorrows, is, by Ishmael's lights, the truest of all men. Immersed in the Beatitudes, Ishmael aspires toward the blessedness of downward mobility while viewing its opposite as a sickness unto death: "All men tragically great are made so through a certain morbidness. Be sure of this, O young ambition, all mortal greatness is but disease."[37]

Presuming oneself the possessor of an absolutely clear head or an anointed knower of good and evil is a genuine threat to democracy and the surest means of being used for wrong and becoming useless for right. This is the self-enclosed imagination of Ahab, mistaking his impulsiveness for integrity, staying the course toward self-destruction:

> The white whale swam before him as the monomaniac incarnation of all those malicious agencies which some deep men feel eating in them, till they are left living on with half a heart and half a lung.
> . . . All that most maddens and torments; all that stirs up the lees of

things; all truth with malice in it; all that cracks the sinews and cakes the brain; all the subtle demonisms of life and thought; all evil, to crazy Ahab, were visibly personified, and made practically assailable in Moby-Dick.[38]

There's a mad simplicity in Ahab's war on terror, and we're all drawn irresistibly toward it as it permeates the herd like a contagion. It would be wonderful if there were no historical deafness involved in saying of the September 11 attacks, "We've never seen this kind of evil before," or if all human malice were conveniently contained in one man, one nation, one terrorist network, or one white whale. But "the face of evil," for all its best-selling simplicity, doesn't actually work that way, and neither evil nor terror are "practically assailable." As an obsessive student of the Bible and Shakespeare, Melville could not imagine otherwise. And like Hawthorne, he understood that hardly anything is more dangerous than a self-satisfied understanding of the Almighty, freedom, good, or evil. To suggest for the cameras or for one's sense of self or for the sake of consumer confidence, that evil is out there, before us in plain view, unrelated to our own history, waiting to be eradicated, is to indulge the speech of the plainly deranged. To evade, in any way, the mendacity that appears to be the native language of humanity will require awareness of this fevered ignorance that inspires our fearful talk and confession of the moral blindness that draws us into the ranks of the insane.

I'll Tickle Your Catastrophe

Following the commercial disaster of *Moby Dick* and the even poorer sales of *Pierre,* Melville delivered an elaborate allegory on the various species of insanity that vie for the position of status quo in American culture. Increasingly estranged from the popular reception that might make writing for a living a possibility, Melville let it all fly in *The Confidence Man,* which features Satan in St. Louis boarding the steamboat *Fidele* (Faithful) bound for New Orleans on April Fools' Day.[39] While the Prince of Darkness plays the confidence man (con man) most aptly, his masquerade only serves to expose the variations of American faith as lesser forms of confidence selling. As a shapeshifter, he will change identity and engage passengers in conversation while representing (or referring to) American optimism, transcendentalism, professional salesmen of Christian faith (Do you *know* Him?), and Indian haters. Reading the novel can be a deeply disconcerting experience, because it becomes difficult to remember with whom the Satan last spoke while trying to keep hold of which of the conversation partners (changing from chapter to chapter) is the Devil. Somehow this seems strangely appropriate.

Within an egocentric and vulnerable American culture, inspiring confidence (or faith in one's faith) is slowly unmasked as the Devil's primary weapon of mass destruction. The faith that is its own justification leads to the violence that believes itself to be liberation and righteousness and always in the service of virtue. Melville dedicates the work "to victims of Auto da Fe,"[40] and the reader will come to understand that confidence (or faith) that is its own referent is inevitably demonic, as victims of mob fury, inquisition, or the scapegoat mechanism will understand all too well. This confidence sucks young blood. Self-confidence, self-respect, and self-faith (in the most absolute sense) will worship nothing so much as its own appetite, an appetite that all too often will be directed by the highest-bidding media presentation, rarely going broke by appealing to the herd instinct and never wavering from the carefully scripted logic of *Vanity Fair.*

The complexity of the prose is such that you can't help but wonder if Melville's already given up hoping that America will receive his prophetic word. To be genuinely faithful to the biblical witness, America will have to temper its egoism with a tragic sensibility and a vigilance against self-delusion lest evil thrive, as evil will, unrecognized. Flannery O'Connor speaks to this danger when she notes that sentimentality that views as unseemly or unpatriotic any real horror of our capacity for self-deception will lead to the gas chamber. She warns against the storytellers' efforts to "tidy up reality" to tickle the readers' (or viewers') ears. Novelists and newsmakers and speechwriters beware.

When Melville, the narrator, steps out from behind the curtain in *The Confidence Man,* he reminds us that reality is hardly done justice by tidying efforts and that a story too tidy is probably, if we haven't already guessed, good news for Satan's kingdom: "That fiction, where every character can, by reason of its consistency, be comprehended at a glance, either exhibits but sections of character, making them appear for wholes, or else is very untrue to reality."[41] Just in case we need reminding, being untrue to reality, to the complexity of actual life, is what propaganda is for, lest we think Melville's simply praising his own incoherence. He's a lover of wisdom who loves truth by knocking down any talk of it as anything less than unfathomable, even if this will require making a moral of the Devil himself. Telling it like it is concerning God and humans will include descriptions of the deeply paradoxical and troubling: "No writer has produced such inconsistent characters as nature herself has."[42]

Television is impatient. The camera lies. And the sound bite, like the headline and the folk ballad, develops in response to the market's demand for information in a particular, digestible form. But the novelist, like the prophet, reminds us that something is rotten with our abstractions and that a God whose wholeness is presumably grasped by a pamphlet, a formula, a commercial, or a pop song is a false god. And when a human being (the bearer of infinite mystery according to the biblical tradition) is summed up by a photo, a bad moment, or a phrase, the essential life of said individual has been slain. To remind us of the meaning of the psalmist's phrase "fearfully and wonderfully made" (Ps. 139:14), Melville brings in the example of the duck-billed beaver (a stumbling block to naturalists of his time) and reminds us that the waters of human nature that can be readily seen through aren't human at all:

> Upon the whole, it might rather be thought, that he, who, in view of its inconsistencies, says of human nature the same that, in view of its contrasts, is said of the divine nature, that it is past finding out, thereby evinces a better appreciation of it than he who, by always representing it in a clear light, leaves it to be inferred that he clearly knows all about it.[43]

Of God and humanity we must not, according to Melville, present ourselves as (or worse, believe ourselves to be) authorities. And to return to Chesterton's observation of America's possibly insane creed, deluding ourselves in this regard, buying the propaganda of collateral damage, "with us or against us," or whatever reductionism serves to justify dehumanization, is unbiblical, unpatriotic, and un-American. Mad Melville felt compelled to compose a stranger fiction than his contemporaries wanted, but in our day, we can receive his testimony on deluding devils, demon possession, and the moral necessity of being bewildered and saying so as an arsenal for democracy. Where there is no bewilderment,we might say, there is no humility, and without humility there can be no understanding, no empathy, and neither liberty nor justice for any.

Dust and Desire

When asked about what book (if any) he'd wished he'd written, William Faulkner didn't hesitate to name *Moby Dick*. And as much as any American writer, Faulkner understood that any literature of the human heart in conflict with itself will be revelatory and, therefore, strange. His work will appear willfully incoherent and odd to minds increasingly unaccustomed to the pleasure of listening to lengthy stories, explanations, arguments, or poetry and increasingly drawn to angry people on television and radio who presume to cobble together answers to all of life's questions in whatever tidying-up manner will keep the most people watching and listening. But the tidying-up impulse can prove toxic, and being true to a wiser American selfhood that can endure and prevail over and against the repeated pressing of the sex, money, and pseudo-patriotic buttons will require familiarizing ourselves anew (or even for the first time) with the ancient wisdom regularly preempted by the sound and fury of the present. As an aspiring resource or vessel for such wisdom, providing a Melvillean counterwitness to the present evil age, Faulkner hoped to, in his words, "scratch the face of the supreme Obliteration and leave a decipherable scar of some sort."[44]

Repeatedly, the wisdom that illuminates Faulkner's haunted American South is the wisdom of America's displaced people. In his appendix to *The Sound and the Fury*, tracing the fortunes of the Compson family into the twentieth century, he begins with Ikkemotubbe ("A dispossessed American king"[45]) whom he describes as "a man of wit and imagination as well as a shrewd judge of character, including his own."[46] A determined, unsparing mindfulness toward one's own intentions, justifications, and troubled inheritance is more than most of Faulkner's characters seem willing to muster, but even those who do, like Ike McCaslin (the protagonist of *Go Down, Moses,* who comes to view Sam Fathers, Ikkemotubbe's descendant, as his mentor), also understand that such mindfulness is rarely articulate: "The heart don't always have time to bother with thinking up words that fit together."[47]

Halfway through *Absalom, Absalom,* Quentin Compson of Mississippi recalls (in his head) the demands of his Harvard roommate, Shreve McCannon: *"Tell about the South. What's it like there. What do they do there. Why do they live there. Why do they live at all."*[48] It is here in the middle that the novel, reading already like an immersion in thick, muddy mystery, almost absent-mindedly recognizes itself as, among other things, one answer to a specific request in the room of a dormitory. Faulkner tells of Compson's hearing tell of Yoknapatawphan legend Thomas Sutpen, but as it proceeds, Compson is doing the telling, and the listening ear moves between Massachusetts and Mississippi in such a hypnotic way that, as one narrator observes, "you cannot know yet whether what you see is what you are looking at or what you are believing."[49] As Faulkner puts down this sort of thing on nearly every page, we have to remind ourselves that he isn't looking to dispense Zen koans or take a turn for the deliberately obscure. He's being descriptive. He's telling about the South and the difficulties of telling and remembering well. And like Shakespeare, his descriptions will often anticipate more than psychology, media studies, and market research have dreamt of in their philosophies.

Faulkner's narrators are free to philosophize over their misperceptions, skewed motivations, and the continuities of consciousness they've inherited from other peoples' stories, explanations, and professions. Nobody gets to get over anybody else, and they're at their worst and most hopeless when they honestly think they can. They're too haunted by one another ever to be free of one another's sayings, mottos, and biblical interpretations. Rearranging our mental furniture to improve our pasts, bettering posterity, and honoring ancestors by simultaneously pushing past their mistaken notions can be a tragically complicated business, but Faulkner's characters are doomed to try any-way. And if his account of our psychological plight is trustworthy, it's made all the more complicated as we appear to be, all of us, fixated on a white whale or two and shamefully self-conscious much of the time. Sizing up the people we've known and loved or hated might be an inevitable habit of the heart, but sitting in the seat of judgment while try-ing to make sense of ourselves can prove to be a damnation all its own. Our minds can't bear the strain. As Cash Bundren of *As I Lay Dying* remarks, "I ain't so sho that ere a man has the right to say what is crazy and what ain't. It's like there was a fellow in every man that's done a-past the sanity or the insanity, that watches the sane and the insane doings of man with the same horror and the same astonishment."[50]

Like Dostoyevsky, Faulkner is a master of what we call the inter-nal monologue, but we have to remind ourselves that the teeming brain was and is *described,* not invented, by the great wordsmiths. We can steer clear of *Notes From Underground,* Hamlet's speeches, and Homer Simpson's innermost thoughts on donuts and beer, but we probably protest too much if we dismiss it all as irrelevant or utterly unlike anything going on in our own heads. We're all stream of con-sciousness now. And given our proneness to judgment, we could do with the occasional vision or descriptive word on how we arrive at what we make of ourselves and each other. As Faulkner writes in *Light in August,* "man knows so little about his fellows. In his eyes all men or women act upon what he believes would motivate him if he were mad enough to do what that other man or woman is doing."[51] In a better world, we might have Faulkner's truisms scrolling along the bottom of our television screens or inscribed on plaques inside the Pentagon. In the meantime, I'd like to offer Faulkner as an American sage who can assist us in the difficult but essential task of thinking about our thinking.

As Melville and Hawthorne demonstrate amply, our projections take on lives of their own apart from the facts on the ground (whether foreign or domestic), and our feverish desires build their own ratio-nale into fixed explanatory grids that are difficult to overcome or imagine our way out of. In Faulkner's fiction, words from the ancient and recent pasts construct these fortresses of solitude in his charac-ters' minds, but they can also liberate, bodying forth lamentation and longing otherwise left unarticulated. In an aspiring democracy, looking hard at our speech and the actions it effects is an ongoing work of moral discernment never unrelated to the role of the storytellers. In *As I Lay Dying*, Addie Bundren thinks back on the words that marked and preceded the turns and twists of her life and, in a mesmerized fashion, notes, "I would think how words go up in a thin line, thick and harmless, and how terribly doing goes along the earth, clinging to it."[52] Melodramatic words and rhetoric are almost inevitably made flesh, in some form or fashion, and Faulkner's talk about talk is a national treasure for the moral development that only comes with a humble determination to watch our language.

Each in Its Ordered Place

As Faulkner understands, our desire for a quick fix, a to-do list, or an easy explanation of whom we're supposed to love and who's most deserving of our wrath is born of a natural need for meaning and order. We want answers and resolution, and we'll pledge allegiance to whatever personality or principality can give it to us the quickest. But when the desire is accelerated or made hasty by the anxiety and fear that electronic media often appears especially designed to provoke, we grow impatient with history and the wisdom it affords by way of its "Once upon a time. . . ." When we're no longer willing (or able) to exercise the attention span required to hear, read, or listen to any version of history that can't be contained in a sound bite or a putdown, our capacity for worship and for contribution to a stable democracy is compromised. To do either, we have to have the skills to understand and locate ourselves not by way of mantras, sayings, and glowing clichés that come to constitute our character, but within a story that's faithful to history. If we're deaf to the oratory of careful, comprehensive storytelling (or even hostile to it), are we still capable of wanting to be truthful?

For instance, a photograph of Donald Rumsfeld shaking hands with Saddam Hussein in 1983 might unsettle a position or provoke an emotional state, but it isn't an argument for or against anyone. It isn't a "bashing." It's simply a record of a historical event, and history isn't a problem for "Once upon a time." Such records invite opinions and positions to explain themselves in the larger context of a history in which tyrants, of course, never spring up out of nowhere as unstoried creatures, and America's relationship with the rest of the world is inevitably more complicated than the daily news has time to let on. It invites us to expand the stories we tell ourselves to include all that comes to our attention as history, not to fight it off as if some rogue element is conspiring to bring down our peace of mind. Remembrance belongs to the people, and Barbara Ehrenreich's account of not getting by on minimum wage isn't a project in slander. It's a testimony. Or as comedian Lenny Bruce never tired of explaining to his fellow citizens, "The truth is what is." Will we believe it?

Almost inevitably, this expansion process will feel painful, because a challenged opinion will often seem like an assault on meaning itself, an assault on meaning by meaninglessness, on order by chaos, on truth by relativism. But it's really just history. More material for the blessed orator. For the mind that strives to order itself according to the biblical witness, turning one's mind around regularly (repentance, metanoia) is the way that leads to everlasting life. While adjusting your imagination to fit the facts on the ground doesn't always inspire confidence or suit the mad self-confidence that tries to pass itself off as respectability (think Chillingworth, Ahab, or any president, CEO, and presumed world leader at one time or another), refusing it as miserable weakness or wishy-washiness is to invite the thought police into your own head—to deny, in advance of hearing it, any facts to the contrary of your frantically held paradigm. Orwell called it Reality Control, and I often wonder if it might be related somehow to blasphemy against the Holy Spirit. We do it to ourselves.

Late one evening in 1928, around the time Faulkner's publisher Ben Wasson had finished working on *Sartoris*, Faulkner dropped off a momentously large envelope. Wasson removed the manuscript and read the title: *The Sound and the Fury*. "This one's the greatest I'll ever write. Just read it,"[53] Faulkner remarked, leaving abruptly. Perhaps as much, or more, than any one work of American literature, this tale of a crumbling household contains multitudes. It is with this work that Faulkner, according to his own testimony, learned to approach words with the alert respect required when handling dynamite. And if Marshall McLuhan was right to define art as anything you can get away with, Faulkner would find that there are some things "to which the shabby term Art, not only can, but must, be applied."[54] There is a blessed and tragic unmanageability at work in the world of which our artless managing of impulses needs reminding.

As a kind of portal into the mental anguish that comes with the failure of life to order itself according to our passionate expectations, the testimonies of the Brothers Compson demonstrate all the ways our faulty pictures hold us captive. They can't quiet their mad minds down, and their opinions, from the outset, seem to matter less and less while their imaginations (Faulkner takes us inside them) begin to feel like pancake batter. But in spite of their fixations, the lived witness of Dilsey, the Compsons' maid, holds together any hope of well-being within the family while also towering over its madness with the promise of a more lasting, humane reality than the Compsons, in their present state of degeneracy, can know or understand.

Long before the advent of either "reality TV" or the soap opera, Faulkner gave us a Quentin Compson who can't stop thinking about his sister Caddy's lost virginity. His obsession with violated honor, injustice, and all that is therefore wrong with the entire world accompanies him to Harvard where he will brood over eternal punishment, the apparent absence of redemption evident in all things, and the option of suicide. He destroys his grandfather's watch that his father bequeathed him, terming it "the mausoleum of all hope and desire."[55] And the voice of southern stoicism he inherited from his father is a cold comfort in his mind as he loses hope in a meaningful future: "No battle is ever won he said. They are not even fought. The field only reveals to man his own folly and despair, and victory is an illusion of philosophers and fools."[56] Half in love with easeful death, he will eventually view all human behavior as "an unvarying nil: stalemate of dust and desire."[57]

Committed to little more than personal acquisition, the gratification afforded him by his visits to prostitutes, and the secret hoarding of money sent long-distance from Caddy for the care and subsistence of a daughter she's only allowed to see with his assistance, Jason Compson is a machine. His mind is a constant rehearsal of who's done him wrong and how everything would fall into place if he was put more officially in charge of all things. Needless to say, he can only feel his own pain, and all he perceives in the sweet old world is the denial of his well-deserved freedom and the assertion of someone else's control. His narration is peppered with such oddly contemporary phrases as "Like I always say," "I don't need any man's help to get along," and "I can stand on my own two feet."[58] Like a good many of us, his head is often filled with all the things he might have said (or might yet say) in various theoretical conversations that end with him victoriously proving his point. There's no telling what he might have done with an Internet hookup. His miserly reduction of all of life to his own needs is never without justification ("I give every man his due, regardless of religion or anything else. I have nothing against jews as an individual. . . . It's just the race"[59]). And he prides himself on his impenetrability to guilt ("I'm glad I haven't got the sort of conscience I've got to nurse like a sick puppy all the time"[60]). As is often the case with personalities who boast of their determination to be "realistic," he will notice nothing out of the ordinary as his supposed pragmatism becomes sadistic, and he becomes progressively perplexed and frightened by the power and endurance of Dilsey.

After Caddy's departure, it is Dilsey and Dilsey alone who esteems the mentally disabled brother Benjy worthy of attentiveness. He's moved mostly by the sight of firelight and the pasture (now a golf course) that was sold to pay for his sister's wedding and his brother Quentin's year at Harvard, where he now listens anxiously to golfers yelling what he takes to be his sister's name. His fetishes are more easily judged and scrutinized by the watching world than those of his brothers, but Faulkner's portrayal of all three can lead the reader to ask who among us is most ultimately handicapped.

The anxiety for order on our own terms, when the facts won't give themselves up so easily to any human mind, is the downfall for each of the novel's male protagonists. And we shouldn't let Faulkner's unconventional way of telling their story obstruct our ability to see ourselves. Something's gone a little funny if we believe William Faulkner or Herman Melville inaccessibly weird while we feel boundless affection for outraged media pundits. We need the orator to get us thinking properly. We need a novel, or at least some comic realism, to help us step back for a moment. *Crossfire* looks a little different on the *Daily Show* when two young girls perform out loud and word for word a transcript of what its adult hosts actually say to each other. We need to get inside the head of a Jason Compson (or a Snopes) to see better what we're in danger of becoming.

When I read Dostoyevsky's *Notes from Underground* with my high school students, I have a difficult time keeping them from dismissing the narrator as a complete lunatic from two centuries ago. But then I invite them to write down, word for word, everything they are told, through word and image, in a single commercial break on the subject of products, politicians, and must-see TV. We then imagine what their own thoughts would look like if the words passing through their minds (unbidden) were somehow projected on a screen for the classroom to see. Gradually, it's easier to see that it isn't Faulkner or Dostoyevsky who are problematic. They only *seem* weird because we've let *Fox News* and *Fear Factor* and the contradictions we house in our heads seem *un*problematic. Perhaps we should hold our tongues a moment longer. Maybe that which we dismiss as "weird" or "obscure" has been stopped short by a defense mechanism. Maybe art is telling us more than we feel prepared to hear. Perhaps that which the man on the screen dismisses with an impatient grimace might actually bear a saving word.

Unvanquished

In a fashion that I can't help but think inspired, in some small way, the image of Irma P. Hall's Marva Munson in the Coens' version of *The Ladykillers,* Dilsey presides as a voice of grace *and* judgment in her long-suffering career with the Compsons. Against the politics that would elevate Jason for his shrewd business sense and marginalize Benjy as an inconvenience, she takes Benjy to her Sunday morning meetings in spite of the local consensus who mumble against the routine as inappropriate and scandalous. "Tell um the good Lawd don't keer whether he smart or not," she retorts. "Don't nobody but poor white trash keer dat."[61]

In a conversation with Caddy over Benjy's changed name (he was initially named after his Uncle Maury until it was discovered that his mind would not develop), Dilsey expresses her disapproval over their decision, insisting that they're buying into the world's wicked ways by thinking him unworthy as a namesake. She notes her own confidence that her name will outlive the confusion of the oppressive and insane present:

> *My name been Dilsey since fore I could remember and it be Dilsey when they's long forgot me.*
>
> *How will they know it's Dilsey, when it's long forgot, Dilsey, Caddy said.*
>
> *It'll be in the Book, honey, Dilsey said. Writ out.*
>
> *Can you read it, Caddy said.*
>
> *Wont have to, Dilsey said. They'll read it for me. All I got to do is say Ise here.*[62]

Thomas Merton once remarked that this is one of the best statements, in all of literature, on the morally subversive vocation of Christian identity. The Jason Compsons of the world will correctly view it as a threat to almost everything they hold dear.

Her procession to the Sunday gathering, with Benjy in tow, is one weekly, palpable manifestation of a life that says, "Ise here." It isn't some spiritual consolation in which she steps back from the rest of life. Hers is an embodied witness that derives from and partakes in the communal witness. The gathering is one of comfort and unburdening and commission to stay the course in expectation of a coming day (that is and was and will be). The visiting reverend from St. Louis plays host to a voice that sinks into the hearts of the congregation "with a sad, timbrous quality like an alto horn" as it broadcasts itself upon the listeners:

> "Brethren and sisteren," it said again. The preacher removed his arm and he began to walk back and forth before the desk, his hands clasped behind him, a meagre figure, hunched over upon itself like that of one long immured in striving with the implacable earth, "I got the recollection and the blood of the lamb!" He stamped steadily back and forth. . . . He was like a worn small rock whelmed by the successive waves of his voice. With his body he seemed to feed the voice that, succubus like, had fleshed its teeth in him. And the congregation seemed to watch with its own eyes while the voice consumed him, until he was nothing and they were nothing

and there was not even a voice but instead their hearts were speaking to one another in chanting measures beyond the need for words, so that when he came to rest against the reading desk . . . a long moaning expulsion of breath rose from them, and a woman's single soprano: "Yes, Jesus!"[63]

As the sermon concludes, Benjy sits "rapt in his sweet blue gaze,"[64] while Dilsey "sat bolt upright beside, crying rigidly and quietly in the annealment and the blood of the remembered Lamb."[65] As she exits the building with tears streaming down her face, her daughter complains,

"Whyn't you quit dat mammy? . . . Wid all dese people lookin. We be passin white folks soon."
"I've seen de first en de last," she says. "Never you mind me."
"First en last whut?" her daughter asks.
"Never you mind. . . . I seed de beginnin, en now I sees de endin."[66]

Like Bayard Sartoris of *The Unvanquished,* who towers over every honor code and overcomes his cultural legacy of an eye for an eye by breaking it down with the offering of his own life, redefining honor in the process, and Ike McCaslin (*Go Down, Moses*) who demonstrates that the Earth is the Lord's and everything in it by refusing the land that is his legal inheritance, offering it instead to his heretofore unacknowledged relatives of mixed race, Dilsey endures. There is a power and a glory beyond the decomposing civilization she finds herself in, and she will bear witness to it by seeking the welfare of her dysfunctional employers while living in watchfulness toward a day that was and is and is to come; a day in which all manner of things will be made well. As visions of enduring, earth-bound liberty (and without them, the people perish), these narratives offer powerful possibilities for the American imagination, and if they're taken to heart, as the best American literature ought to be, Faulkner might well have left a decipherable scar or two on the face of Obliteration. As the storyteller will do, he deconstructs the death-dealing, decrepit notions of honor and glory by telling better tales, redeeming the old dispensations by challenging our sense of ignorant ease. Great literature does that.

Keep Cool, But Care

While Thomas Pynchon probably owes more to the Beat movement than to the visions of Faulkner, his attentiveness to history and the details of the contemporary American scene (a hyperawareness that sees revelation in progress all around him and a parable to be entered into around every corner) places him appropriately along our continuum of moral voices. As a kind of visionary, grounded yet awake to mystery in all things, his unique brand of watchfulness reflects a love for the American landscape and the countercultural possibilities still at work, though often untapped, within the national character. He looks hard and humorously at everything we're becoming with an eye for every virus of unfreedom that might corrupt our cultural imagination. He seems particularly interested in all the ways in which a principality will kid itself concerning its own history (recent and ancient) and all the madness that inevitably follows. If the price of liberty is eternal vigilance against unstoried tyranny and death-dealing impulses played out as necessities, Pynchon's patriotism involves enough overtime to leave his readers feeling dizzy. But the charges of pessimism and paranoia often leveled at those who deem the practice of paying attention a civic duty are unfair, and in Pynchon's case, betray a misunderstanding (purposeful?) of what he's up to.

The motto "Keep Cool, but Care" is viewed by many of Pynchon's readers as a theme within his first novel, V., that can also serve as a guiding ethos throughout his fiction.[67] It's uttered by McClintic Sphere who, depending on your interpretation, might be viewed as a stand-in for Ornette Coleman or Thelonious Monk, and it's an increasingly necessary word for reading Pynchon as you come to suspect he's never met a conspiracy theory he didn't like. It speaks against the cynicism of ignorant bliss as well as for the desire to know history even as you're troubled by it. As Fred Friendly understood, learning to live with the tension of what you'd rather not have known concerning the interconnectedness of the workaday world is the beginning of wisdom. While delving further always puts one at risk of entering a territory of defeat, loss of meaning, and powerlessness, joy that depends on an aloof posture of disregard for the actual world appears to be, in Pynchon's view, a poor showing for the promise of America. Trying to care against despair will involve, among other things, a determined wit that can overcome melancholy, a turn for the comedic that won't let tragedy have the final word. Incidentally, comic consistency, in Pynchon's work, is a conspiracy of hope requiring constant satirization of the merry band of resisters who appear throughout his novels. In *Vineland,* for instance, his liberation force concludes a planning session, ready to tackle fascism and every form of totalitarian thought encroaching upon the realm of liberty, and the moment they get up coincides with the theme from *Ghostbusters* suddenly breaking out on a nearby radio. Every moment of emerging seriousness eventually finds itself in a larger comic context, a funnier parable than whatever gravitas momentarily held the stage.

When Pynchon terms his resistance movements (against "Them") the Counterforce or the People's Republic of Rock 'n' Roll, he can bring to mind the odd, moral authority of Jack Black or Lear's Fool or Tom Bombadil. As absolute power corrupts absolutely, it becomes increasingly intolerant of the playful word and the honest though powerless testimony. In *Vineland,* Pynchon's freedom fighters believe that corrupting power keeps "a log of its progress, written into that most sensitive memory device, the human face,"[68] and filming the unsympathetic powerful, with an emphasis on the close-up, will dethrone and unmask them slowly but surely. The subject of his lamentation and the object of his lampoon is whatever comes only to steal and destroy, seeking whom it may devour, inevitably appearing to its host bodies (Pynchon's "They") as an absolute moral necessity, duty, what-we-have-to-do, doublethink. Naming the Adversary ("the persistence of structures favoring death. . . . This is the sign of Death the impersonator"[69]), mocking power and speaking truth to it, would seem to be the purpose that, in some way, links all of his work. Celebration of life, not letting the Caesars or multinational cartels or whoever talks most loudly and expensively about freedom define who you are, is the driving method of a prose that kicks at the darkness. It's cynicism's opposite: coolness and caring.

As the Beats and the biblical witness remind us, a nervous breakdown is at large, advertising itself as normalcy, and that which gets called sanity might sometimes be nothing more than the agreed-on madness of the powerful. Pynchon's characters represent a humankind who can't bear much manufactured reality, and their inability to fit in or get with the program begins to look like a much-beleaguered stronghold of freedom. In our collection of stories, our patchwork fit for discipleship and democracy, we can note that Hawthorne and Melville have taken us here before. There is a contagion of power and pride and endless self-justification that will spread out in every direction, disguising itself as something to which anyone with any sense of decency would have to submit. The warped wood of human nature won't produce the righteousness of God on earth, but it thinks it will. It believes in its own sincerity so powerfully that it will feel violently offended at any question concerning its well-rehearsed script of goodness and sacrifice in all that it does, in all that it's ever done. It will mistake its Towers of Babel (cooperatives of concentrated lies) for the light that shines in the darkness.

To describe much of what we call history as a diversionary tactic or "at best a conspiracy, not always among gentlemen, to defraud" is to bring biblical insight to bear on the way we think about the past.[70] It is to stand firmly within the Jewish Christian tradition and its teaching that evil doesn't come to us self-consciously, introducing itself and offering us a choice ("Join us in our evil"). It's more like a kind of sleepwalking, an unself-consciously Faustian bargain, a narcissism in which we believe our fantasy to be the only real, unbiased version of events. We surround ourselves with voices that will affirm our fantasy and dismiss as treacherous (or evil) any witness that would dare to call our innocence into question. And if the human heart is deceitful above all else, we will often be tempted to believe and anxiously defend our most complicated pretensions.

As Thoreau, Tolstoy, Gandhi, and Martin Luther King Jr. insisted, combatting evil in all its impersonations will begin with a refusal to cooperate with it. In *Gravity's Rainbow*, Pynchon notes that evil will usually assume a "calculated innocence" ("It's part of Their style"[71]), and the ancient curse of Western culture is its "dusty Dracularity" made all the more inimical by its ability to publicize itself as Progress, "even to the point of masquerading, a bit decadently, as mercy."[72] Taking the power of collective delusion seriously, Pynchon follows the lead of Allen Ginsberg, who noted that the high places of Baal and the logic of human sacrifice to Moloch aren't limited to biblical history. Like Hawthorne and Melville, Pynchon locates unacknowledged alliances with unholiness close to home. And like Emily Dickinson, he understands that our failures aren't compressed in an instant. They're consecutive and slow and well-intentioned, and tracing them well, the comedy and tragedy of it all, will require some careful storytelling, fair and balanced reportage, and some redemptively meandering confabulation. Above all, tracing our world out truthfully will involve salvific doubt concerning our ability to know and the abandonment of domineering knowingness for the more biblical justness that only lives by faith. Cultural revolutions are always housed in stories. Revolution *is* story. It will be told. "Once upon a time. . . ." "The kingdom of God is like. . . ." Enter Reverend Cherrycoke.

Tell It Slant

Among the numerous characters who come and go in *Gravity's Rainbow* is an unnamed German girl who spends an evening with the novel's confused American protagonist, Tyrone Slothrop, who's found himself wandering around postwar Germany in a pig costume. Their conversation turns to the topic of her father, a printer, missing since 1942, whose union had resisted the Nazis while all the others were getting dutifully in line. The tale of his existence inspires a state of freedom-loving reverie in Slothrop as he contemplates the commitment of his Puritan forebears who dared to speak and write down the truth as they understood it, in spite of persecution. He also considers the possibilities of warring on terror with a printing press: "It touches Slothrop's own Puritan hopes for the Word, the Word made printer's ink, dwelling along with antibodies and iron-bound breath in a good man's blood . . . did he run off leaflets against his country's insanity? was he busted, beaten, killed?"[73]

Exiled to a pre-1776 America in response to similar crimes against authority, we have the Reverend Wicks Cherrycoke as our primary narrator and spirit guide in Pynchon's latest novel, *Mason & Dixon*. Charged by the British with the crime of "Anonymity,"[74] Cherrycoke was discovered printing and posting unsigned flyers outlining injustices he'd observed, "committed by the Stronger against the Weaker."[75] He'd named the guilty and been locked up, and as he began to protest the notion that his own name, not his to give or withhold according to the law, belonged to the British authorities, he was declared insane ("or so, then, each in his Interest, did it please ev'ryone to style me"[76]) and shipped off to the New World for treatment.

Just in case we need reminding, it is the Hebrew scribe (not the hippy or the Marxist) who first announced that the mouths of liars will be stopped, that the one who oppresses the weak despises the Maker, and that the Lord opposes the proud but gives grace to the humble. It is the Bible that gives a voice of moral authority to the refugee, viewing the disenfranchised as the custodians of truthfulness. Excommunicated for his own commitment to truth and justice, Cherrycoke, an American Baron Munchausen, holds forth in the household of his sister and her husband, John Wade LeSpark, a weapons merchant who's made his fortune selling arms "to French and British, Settlers and Indians alike."[77] The Reverend is allowed to subsist with the LeSparks as long as he keeps the children amused with stories. His audience will include LeSpark's brothers and their children as well. The year is 1786, and the place is Philadelphia.

Cherrycoke is an expert in circumlocution. Truth, as he sees it, demands as much. Like wisdom, it will have to dazzle gradually. He'll tell it slant. Easing it with explanation, he spins his yarns "for their moral usefulness."[78] But as the properly received parable will often dislocate (rather than reinforce) the personal peace of mind of the hearer, exposing the ways we go about betraying our most publicized values, it shouldn't surprise us to find that the Reverend is ever a prophet without honor, possibly too much the enemy of the state for his family's tastes, and the charge of insanity will continue to be placed in his direction by those whose interests are threatened by his truth telling.

Needless to say, the family values that come through in the conversational storytelling that constitutes the novel do not always coincide with one another. Given the fact that arbitrary weapons sales fuel the LeSparks' household economy, young nephew Ethelmer imagines that "if there are Account-books in which Casualties are the Units of Exchange . . . his Uncle is deeply in Arrears."[79] But Pynchon's Pennsylvanians have yet to lose the art of listening to one another or putting questions and answers tactfully, and all are reluctant to directly insult their host. While Cherrycoke is inarguably a man of faith, he understands that LeSpark's devotion to the notions of Adam Smith are no less a faith-based initiative than his own vocation. As he sees it, LeSpark lives "safe inside a belief as unquestioning as in any form of Pietism you could find,"[80] and his travels as an arms dealer are performed "under the protection of a superior Power,—not, in this case, God, but rather Business. What turn of earthly history, however perverse, would dare interfere with the workings of the Invisible Hand?"[81] Although it is Cherrycoke's own version of America that has the floor, he knows that he lives in close proximity to LeSpark's regime, which thrives everywhere unnamed, understanding itself by way of "undeclared secular terms in the Equations of Proprietary Happiness."[82]

The Legacy Was America

Twenty years after the fact, Cherrycoke tells the tale of a line he witnessed and how it was put straight through the heart of a wilderness. In his account, Charles Mason and Jeremiah Dixon function as the Rosencrantz and Guildenstern of the Age of Reason, following their orders as duty seems to require while wondering if there's any particular duty motivating the Charter'd Companies (Factory, Consulate, Agency) whose interests are consistently served by the work they've undertaken on behalf of the Royal Society. "Charter'd Companies may indeed be the form the World has now increasingly begun to take,"[83] Mason remarks somewhat regretfully while wondering if the benefit of hindsight might transform his actions. Can we ever know completely what ends we're serving? Dixon notes that erring comes with being a human in history, but folly can occasionally be curbed by the presence of "a Remembrancer, as some would say a Conscience."[84] As a Quaker, Dixon believes such mindfulness is accessed through silence in worship, a wisdom beyond the immediate evidence of our eyes and memories, but Mason doesn't quite see the point of mixing up their jobs with "Religious Matters."[85] Like many future citizens of the land he's unwittingly defining, he suspects he knows how to step back from religion when there's a job to do.

"Are we being us'd by Forces invisible?"[86] Dixon fondly asks. And as a novel about science, technology, and cartography, the story leads us to wonder if the surveyor of land might prove to be, biblically speaking, the purveyor of mass delusions. Reverend Cherrycoke accords the right of division to God who, he notes, did well to divide the waters with the firmament. But he wonders if the manmade divisions that follow aren't sometimes a little presumptuous, a machinery that claims Authority without the proper reverence for the glory of God in nature and human beings. Having narrowly escaped the fading, secularized lights of Europe, he hopes for the epiphanies of American Illumination, viewing the land as "a Prairie of Desperate Immensity."[87]

As storyteller and Remembrancer, Cherrycoke places his characters in the company of various movers and shakers on the eve of the republic's founding. When Dixon drinks a toast to "the pursuit of happiness,"[88] a young Thomas Jefferson asks if he might borrow the phrase. They'll encounter Washington and Franklin on their journey as well, but the America that Cherrycoke celebrates is "the America of the Soul" lying beyond the presumption of deism and the arrogance of enlightenment "into an Interior unmapp'd."[89] It is for this, a countercultural, unmapped world of Word made flesh in spite of the domineering claims of royalty or a corrupt Christendom, that the Reverend printed and posted his fliers in the first place. His America serves as "a very Rubbish-Tip for subjunctive hopes, for all that *may yet be true*."[90] But there is also a spirit of reduction and devastation at work "that slowly triangulates its Way into the Continent, changing all from subjunctive to declarative, reducing Possibilities to Simplicities that serve the ends of Governments."[91] This, he fears, will win away the New World "from the Realm of the Sacred."[92] And as the experience of Mason and Dixon demonstrates, this demystifying machinery was doing its business some time before 1776.

Having witnessed the horrors of the slave trade during a visit to the Cape of Good Hope and their arrival in Maryland (not unrelated to the notion of Proprietary Happiness), Mason and Dixon begin to see a pattern at work in Lancaster, Pennsylvania, where an Indian massacre had occurred. They find it peculiar that "the first mortal acts of Savagery in America after their Arrival should have been committed by Whites against Indians,"[93] and they're dismayed by the manner in which the settlers "are become the very Savages of their own worst Dreams, far out of Measure to any Provocation."[94] While otherwise priding himself on his dedicated participation in the Age of Reason, Mason is moved to pray at the site of the massacre, "like a Nun before a Shrine,"[95] as he later described the moment to Dixon. And as he prays, he experiences a troubled premonition concerning future generations whose skills in remembering well might prove woefully diminished: "In Time, these People are able to forget ev'rything. Be willing but to wait a little, and ye may gull them again and again."[96]

As they anticipate an engagement with representatives of the Mohawk nation, they're prepared to answer any number of questions about their strange instruments, but they come to dread the possibility that anyone would put the more straightforward query, "Why are you doing this?"[97] The undeclared, secular terms haunt them as they progressively doubt whether or not their roles are for the good. "Whom are we working for, Mason?" Mason: "I rather thought, one day, you would be the one to tell me."[98]

Making History

Cherrycoke's biblical distrust of concentrated, unchecked power marks his revolutionary Americanness. And as he tells this story of the Founding (or as some Pynchon readers put it, the Anti-Founding), his listeners, especially the older LeSparks, are continually put off by what they take to be his bias. But bias is as difficult to prove as objectivity, and those who claim to be the most fair and balanced in their reportage, like those who would boast of their humility or sincerity, undermine their own claims. Truth, like beauty, is its own credential. Like wisdom, truthfulness doesn't go about promoting itself. It cries out in the street, raising its voice in the marketplace, extending its hand, but it can't exactly heed itself or force anyone else to heed. It will only witness and testify. Like poetry, it doesn't *make* anything happen. Ethelmer listens to the Reverend and the

LeSparks' protestations and smiles as if to say, "We are surrounded by the Pious, and their well-known wish never to hear anything that sets the Blood a-racing."[99] They're uncomfortable with words that might challenge them to care more or think differently.

Cherrycoke aspires to truthfulness, but he knows that claiming to own it is a heresy (Who can know the mind of God?), and believing yourself capable of seeing it undimly is a crime against humanity: "Who claims Truth, Truth abandons. History is hir'd, or coerc'd, only in Interests that must ever prove base."[100] Cherrycoke was run out of old Europe for his stand concerning the "Authorial Authority"[101] of one human voice that aspired to speak to the people for the people. And the beauty of witness is that it doesn't come with signs and wonders. In the land of Cherrycoke's dream, it is freely given and freely ignored. Let anyone who has an ear hear. Keep cool, but care.

On *The Simpsons,* when Montgomery C. Burns, threatened by the ability of Springfield's citizens to make of him what they will, decrees the age of his own first-person singular by crowning himself king of all media, Lisa Simpson, in typical American fashion, procures her own printing press and goes to work on the Red Dress Press. In spite of the manufactured controversies of a Burns-directed media, young Lisa will craft her own versions of the way things are, a prophetic consciousness concerning what's important. This is what American storytellers, from Hawthorne to Pynchon, have always done. Alternative storytelling is underway. And "Authorial Authority" is once again asserted as a human right. Or, if you like, America is founded on revolution all over again. *Semper Reformanda.*

Predictably, Burns cracks down on her operation without mercy, but it's too late. Cherrycoke is contagious. Lenny, Barney, Flanders, and all of Springfield are following suit. Echoing Martin Luther, Homer remarks, "Instead of one big-shot controlling all the media, now there's a thousand freaks Xeroxing their worthless opinions." So be it. This is the way the work gets done in the land of a thousand freaks. Let freedom ring. And blessed be the name of the Lord. Remembrance, after all, belongs to the people.

Chapter 4

Bloodier Than Blood:
Risking All on Resurrection

*Slang, profoundly considr'd, is the lawless germinal ele-
ment, below all words and sentences, and behind all poetry,
and proves a certain perennial rankness and protestantism in
speech.*
                                                      —*Walt Whitman*

Lifelessness is the Great Enemy & always wears a hip-guard.
                                                      —*Bob Dylan*

It sounds like we're all drunks settin' in the house singin' this.
—*Loretta Lynn on recording* Van Lear Rose *with Jack White*

*Honest is a strange word. By definition, if you're going to get
up onstage and sing songs then you're probably pretty bogus.*
                                                      —*Peter Buck*

*T*he joys of trying to think historically about America are especially
evident in any consideration of the stories and roots and diversions
that make up American music. Trying to trace continuums and influences is a deeply edifying and engrossing guesswork of who heard
what when and how exactly it hit them when it came their way. What
all happened in the two thousand or so years between the death of
Jesus outside of Jerusalem and Tom Waits's mad, howling performance of "Jesus Gonna Be Here" on an album called *Bone Machine*?
Is he thinking of Blind Willie Johnson? How exactly did he find himself singing like that? What's he trying to do? What's the history?
   Phrases like "old, weird America" and "the secret history of rock

'n' roll" seem to distinguish the obsessives from the casual music listener. There is much discussion, for instance, on the matter of whether it was Ann Cole of Newark, New Jersey, or Muddy Waters of Rolling Fork, Mississippi, who first broached the topic of getting one's mojo working. Did Elvis ever hear the Golden Gate Jubilee Quartet's lively praise song "Rock My Soul" of 1938? What's with Screamin' Jay Hawkins singing about a little demon running through the world in an effort to understand his own pain? And where does Roy Orbison fit into all this mess? Does it get any weirder than "In Dreams"?

Actually it does. And again, weirdness is only that which has yet to find a slot within our categories and paradigms, and maybe nothing human ever should. If America is a nation of outcasts, castoffs, and hijacked bloodlines, the "authorial authority" of many a troubled voice, blue with longing and crying passionately for change, will characterize our music. While performing alongside Lucinda Williams, Elvis Costello wondered aloud concerning the uselessness of many musical categories and noted that "folk music" is an especially strange one; "music for folks" covers an awfully broad range.

Folks tell of their experiences and of stories they've heard, and the "I feel like . . ." can go absolutely anywhere: a stranger in your own house, a motherless child, a walking contradiction. And the songs aren't necessarily hidden ways of saying something else. They're their own brand of saying. Like the Psalms, they don't contain principles or ideologies but are attempts at truthful witness and testimony. They're just saying how it feels and what happened and wondering if it had to go that way. The world seems to be falling apart; something's got to give, and there is plenty to tell of passion, guilt, oppression, and perplexity in the meantime. It takes a worried man. There are heartaches by the number. And nobody has to look too far to spot a cheating heart or two. There's a riot going on. Or as Dolly Parton puts it, "It's All Wrong but It's Alright."

The Table Is Spread

In this sense, gospel is a wider-ranging culture than we tend to imagine. It might be inevitable that the term would be used for advertising, but that doesn't mean we have to let it be so defined. When we think of the Bible as "religion" or "spirituality," we're letting ourselves be misled if we think primarily of consistently "uplifting" verses or devotional thoughts inscribed on greeting cards or written in tracts. There is a place for the encouraging word, and it is so sweet to trust in Jesus, but the biblical witness is a little muddier than the "spirituality" market usually allows. More than a book of doctrines or "thoughts for the day," the Bible is lamentation and longing and wondering (sometimes hopeful) about what God has in mind. It broadens the doors of perception. The witness is a blessed assurance certainly, but it doesn't close the door to questions and plaintive expression. The "How long?" is in close proximity to the "Lord, come quickly." And a determined trust in the Maker's goodness makes room for the truthful, embarrassing testimony that we're sometimes so lonesome we could die.

This is, in large part, a blues sensibility. The hope of consolation might draw out a song, but the singer need not pretend to be definitively consoled. And a feigned comfort, like a faked assurance, is an anxious hype from which the blues spirit will flee. We can't always see too well when we're trying to look good, coerce cheer, or convince the watching world that we couldn't be happier. The biblical call to speak truthfully (of joy *and* sorrow) is a deliverance from pretension and the defensive optimism that our false gods insist on, a freeing up from enslavement to appearances. You have to lose your life to find it. We don't become honest or true or relaxed overnight, and that's all right. We don't have to candy-coat the hard times. We can sing with Charley Patton, "Lord I'm Disturbed" (1929) and believe with Bukka White "I'm in the Heavenly Way" (1930). There's room for both at the same time. There has to be. It's biblical.

If we think of the expression "gospel truth" as good news truth or kingdom-coming truth, we might begin to understand the eschatological ("end times") significance of the American music under discussion. And it should be said that the "end times" element of the music isn't a strictly premillenial hope of a Jesus who will return and personally thank particular individuals for always looking after Jerusalem's borders and say unto the Pentagon, "Well done my good and faithful servant." It speaks to the public and the private, our hearts and our spending habits, the home and the landscape of international relations. The gospel truth woven throughout the music is the insistence that "A Change Is Gonna Come," and it will be a severe and blessed reversal of fortunes. Things are about to turn around. All oppression shall cease. Weapons systems will be beaten into plowshares. Senseless pain, death, foreclosures, and crop failure can now be talked about with candor and passion and amusement. A place is made for telling it like it is—what Melville called a "democratic dignity."

With the power of Herod, Pilate, Jim Crow, and Pharaoh somehow relativized, the music is free to operate under the assumption that the just prerogatives of the Almighty will somehow ultimately prevail. The avenues for communication (of fear, worry, hope, and gospel) are expanded into a great wide open. And here again, the dissent and truth telling of those about to rock and roll can't quite be characterized by the religious/political, sacred/secular supposed dichotomies. We might just as well insist that William Blake's visions were either religious *or* political. When Sister O. M. Terrell declares matter-of-factly that if the Bible's right, somebody's wrong (in 1953 with a guitar sound that anticipates Jimmy Page and a distinctly Little Richard-like howl), the powers that be are put on high alert. The whole human and all of society are engaged with a mystical, prophetic power that knows no convenient divisions. The times are going to change.

In a wonderful, provocatively messy meditation called *Mumbo Jumbo,* Ishmael Reed describes the elusive quality of jazz/blues/freedom-chime-that-got-Elvis-moving as "Jes Grew." The phrase comes from James Weldon Johnson's description of a "jes' grew" song: "It was a song that had been sung for years through the South. The words were unprintable, but the tune was irresistible, and it belonged to nobody."[1] For Reed, the "Jes Grew" factor is the redemptive cultural practice of "HooDooing the dice" to make them roll sevens every time, a sneaking in of good cheer and hilarity to deconstruct the trouble of troubled times.[2] It isn't always received as good news by the gatekeepers ("Cut out this Jes Grew that keeps a working man up to all hours of the night with its carryings on. The Ballyhoo of its Whoopie. Its Cab Calloway hidihidiho"[3]), but it's a salt that's kept its saltiness, a mustard seed that contains multitudes. It's a kind of liberating virus, spreading like a contagion through cul-

ture and undoing death-dealing seriousness and defensive posturing
wherever it lurks:

> *They did not understand that Jes Grew was unlike physical plagues.*
> *Actually Jes Grew was anti-plague. Some plagues caused the body*
> *to waste away; Jes Grew enlivened the host. Other plagues were*
> *accompanied by bad air (malaria). Jes Grew victims said that the*
> *air was as clear as they had ever seen it and that there was the aroma*
> *of roses and perfumes which had never before enticed their nostrils.*
> *Some plagues arise from decomposing animals, but Jes Grew is elec-*
> *tric as life and is characterized by ebullience and ecstasy.*[4]

The transmission of Jes Grew broadens the range of human
expression. It teaches us how to keep cool and care. It belittles our
idols and channels stories of suffering and hope that remind us we
aren't strangers to other people's prayers. And Easter becomes a big-
ger reality than the oppressive present.

The Slow Holy Train

There are compilations and PBS series and folk music anthologies, and
they're all good, but an especially strong sampling of "anti-plague" in
a box, a document tracing its squeeze through certain cracks, would
have to be the *Goodbye, Babylon* collection. David Fricke calls it a
"box of holy ruckus," and Greil Marcus terms it "country-religious
music." But really, what isn't? Is there even such a thing as "secular"
here? I suppose an older generation might have referred to it as "human
interest," but I prefer Melville's "multiple pilgrim species." In a
wooden box with an engraving of Gustav Dore's Tower of Babel, we
have five CDs with 135 songs (1902–60) placing the Louvin Brothers
and Hank Williams right in there with Mahalia Jackson, Jaybird Coleman, Skip James ("Jesus Is A Mighty Good Leader"), and Charles
Butts Sacred Harp Singers. It's a living witness to what Flannery
O'Connor's Misfit observed with a note of disapproval and frustration:
"Jesus thrown everything off balance."[5] This mystical, earthbound
hodgepodge is the vision of Lance Ledbetter of Atlanta, Georgia, and
he even throws in a CD of twenty-five sermons (1926–41) featuring

Rev. Webb's "Moses Was Rescued by a Negro Woman," Elder Otis Jones's "O Lord I'm Your Child," and (my favorite) Rev. J. M. Gates's "Death Might Be Your Santa Claus." When you hear the call and response, the accelerations and the euphoria, and oft-repeated phrases, like "In the midnight hour" and "Take me to the river," our boundaries concerning popular music and its origins begin to appear not only ineffective, but inappropriate and out of hand. Irreverent even.

"Some of these days" is the operative phrase. Blind Willie Johnson can't keep from crying sometimes, but the Lord will bear all burdens away. And there is a train and a river and a light coming down. "Some of these days" characterizes an age to come that will further sanctify an already sacramental present. The tension between what is and what ought to be drives the growls against hypocrisy and the satirization of the self-satisfied and uptight. Even the ostensibly "religious" (entranced by the appearance of righteousness) get kicked around and lifted up by an unbound holiness. If there's a justice that will still all lying tongues and a day when the dead and the rubbed out will return to tell a story or two, all speech is up for grabs. Nobody gets the copyright on truth or eternity. None are forever silenced. Coercively convincing Babylon is fallen. Intimidation is temporary. There'll be no more sorrows once the roll is called.

In discussions of Charley Patton, Robert Johnson, and Mississippi John Hurt, the term "mother wit" is sometimes used to describe a fanciful, authority-deriding, improvised oratory that inhabited the displaced communities out of which these figures emerged. Like Jes Grew, it makes louder and livelier expression permissible and appropriate, a way of staring down madness with mirth. There is no terrain outside its jurisdiction, no subject that's inappropriate or irrelevant to its stories and sayings, its way of bringing light to those who walk in darkness and disaster and lovesickness.

In "Daniel Saw the Stone" (1931), the Silver Leaf Quartette of Norfolk describe a historical momentum that begins with Daniel staying the wrath of King Nebuchadnezzer against the wise men of Babylon by giving a description and an interpretation of the king's restless dream. The vision is that of a rolling stone, hewn out of a mountain and not made by human hands, which breaks through Babylon, becomes a mountain, and fills the entire earth. As the Silver

Leaf Quartette sing it, a young David as well as Jesus got hold of the same stone, and now they, with their families, want to get hold of it too. The stone, turned mountain, turned inheritor of earth, is the only game in town. Call it what you like. This rolling stone breaks down crowns and thrones and all that oppresses, and it somehow encompasses all good, drawing in and redeeming all manner of things, making them well and whole.

Experiments in Telling the Truth

If the hope of the rolling stone is to be a *complete orientation* (a whole life ethic and a seamless garment), it will have to evade marginalization by that which boasts of itself as the "real world" and refuse the straitjacket of commodification. It has to reintroduce itself to the cultures formed out of it lest they assume they have it all down pat ("You have heard it said. . . . But I say . . ."). It's a matter of constant renovation and reform. "What do these Knaves mean by Virtue?"[6] asks William Blake of the minds of official Christendom. Would the Hebrew prophets recognize in European "Virtue" anything resembling the unshackled hope of the living God? What abstractions are serving to gag the Holy Spirit? Woody Guthrie seeks out the ancient paths when he wonders what Jesus would make of America ("Jesus Christ") and what America would really make of him. And when he nominates Jesus for the office of president of the United States (expertly put to music, incidentally, by Wilco and Billy Bragg), he's contemplating another faithful variation on this blessed theme, a comic joy that speaks prophetically to the concrete world.

On Woody Guthrie's guitar is inscribed the warning "This machine kills fascists," and this sensibility isn't limited to what was termed "folk" or "protest music." The fifties experienced a less easily categorized culture of Total Information Awareness. Wide-eyed Little Richard would boast of a healing to make the dumb and deaf hear and talk, and a young man named Bobby Zimmerman of Hibbing, Minnesota, would long to join his band. Ginsberg and Burroughs would talk of glory in the gutter in an attempt to heal the spirit of America. The lonelyhearts club voices were everywhere. Roy Orbison donned dark glasses and cried out loud over unrequited love in a majestic, near-operatic pop. Jack Kerouac would wander the country writing it all down and telling it like it is. Disruptive truthfulness hit the streets in the land of shaken nerves and rattled brains.

For his part, Johnny Cash said he was pleased to channel "voices that were ignored or even suppressed in the entertainment media, not to mention the political and educational establishments."[7] For Jes Grew, there are no subhumans ~~ ~~~ ' fools. And anyone who aspires to o   t take back its invi-tation to all who   hised, mostly unin-vited souls, with   table to its flow. If it's by our own i   afford to measure without mercy? '   ir, no further"? In speaking truth to   tes us into a larger authenticity than   ustomed. It won't pause to be est   ...ways too far ahead to be respectable. The Love Supreme outshines all lesser loves.

Within three weeks of the assassination of John F. Kennedy, a slightly intoxicated Bob Dylan was invited to speechify upon receiving the Tom Paine award at a fund-raising dinner put on by the Emergency Civil Liberties Committee commemorating Bill of Rights Day. After remarking that the audience should probably spend more time relaxing on the beach, he referenced Woody Guthrie (an idol for both Dylan and his well-dressed audience) and spoke dismissively of the notion that any person or gathering could claim to speak definitively on behalf of other people: "I've never seen one history book that tells how anybody feels."[8] A reasonable enough sentiment for a twenty-two-year-old guitar wielder, but he went on to remark about the confusion and fear of the times, the loneliness and estrangement that a man can't help but feel, and the understanding that can't come without empathy. Taking it as a given that such empathy was the perceived task of the people in front of him (and probably that of any artist worthy of the title), he went on to express a word of pity (an "I can relate") for the most on-his-own-with-no-direction-home figure of the day, one Lee Harvey Oswald.

To say the least, this did not go over very well. And after the boos and an explanatory profile in *The New Yorker* ("Those people that night were actually getting me to look at colored people as colored people. . . . What's wrong goes much deeper than the bomb. What's wrong is how few people are free"[9]). The chimes of freedom, it appeared, weren't to extend so far as to speak to the troubled soul of Public Enemy Number One. The Great Enemy of Unsympathy had just unmasked itself as it lurked in the heart of the liberal establishment. Dylan reminded the audience that peace, love, and understanding have to have an actual object; that abstractions (the poor, the uneducated, the dispossessed) won't do. The Baptist civil rights advocate Will Campbell would also receive flack, around the same time, when he insisted that radically reverent love be extended to the Klansmen, loving them and praying for them as the New Testament demands. But we don't always like to be reminded of certain unfulfilled obligations and possibilities. We forget that the politics of exclusion aren't solely practiced by the "opposition." There's more than one way to be prejudiced. Must there always be scapegoats?

The stone that rolled through Babylon is always farther along than any person or group who would presume to speak on its behalf. When it's in danger of a pendulum swing too far away from one end of the multiple pilgrim species, a possible corrective (for anyone with an ear to hear) comes up on the airwaves. Take Merle Haggard's "Okie From Muskogee" (1969), which dares to lampoon the conformity of "nonconformity" while also envisioning a liberating space, an even broader America where "even squares can have a ball." Who's being kept in the margins now? Are there some who can never hope for a backstage pass? Has "free love" generated its own snooty unfreedom? Is everybody really welcome? Will the circle be unbroken?

Fixtures and Forces and Friends

After the Bill of Rights Day fiasco, Dylan would no longer indulge much in the way of public speaking or any close affiliation with any organization with an axe to grind. It wasn't a step away from the political or the topical, but the work would have to speak for itself. The rolling stone won't abide formalization. And any effort to categorize it as high art or low, folk or rock, spiritual or worldly would be dismissed as part of the soul-sucking establishment's attempt to debilitate it or, as Dylan put it in a short-lived *Hootenanny* column, "boundary it all up."[10]

Taking the music seriously, living within it, and making it your own (without troubling yourself with whether you're country, Beat, hipster, gospel, hip-hop, or rock 'n' roll) is a vocation sufficient unto itself. Opening yourself up to the music and all its sociocultural possibilities involves a receptivity toward more than the market or any brand officialdom can know or understand. There's something more wonderful, open-ended, risky, and unyielding going on. As Dylan describes the music, "it's weird, full of legend, myth, Bible and ghosts . . . chaos, watermelons, clocks, everything."[11] Its truthfulness scandalizes, sanctifies, and enlivens every scene. Like the Bible, the music imaginatively dismantles structures of sorrow, oppression, hypocrisy, and enslavement. The liberating word won't be boundaried.

Regrettably, the "folk" community itself was uncomfortable with Dylan's unwillingness to confine his music to any either/or. Working out one's own vocation with fear and trembling will involve resisting the compartments of marketeers, sociologists, and uptight colleagues. *Another Side of Bob Dylan* (released in May of 1964) places such civil rights–era anthems as "Chimes of Freedom" right alongside "All I Really Want To Do." And "To Ramona" observes that the stratagems of unfreedom will defy easy description as sorrows stem by way of "fixtures and forces and friends," hyping and objectifying to enforce groupthink and deadened visions.

Having already burned a bridge or two with his ill-timed word of solidarity for Lee Harvey Oswald, with *Another Side* Dylan received a cool reception from the folk music community, who, in turn, received a prophetic word from Johnny Cash in a letter to the editors of *Sing Out!*: "SHUT UP! . . . AND LET HIM SING!"[12] (Sidenote: Dylan recently remarked that he still has his copy of that particular issue.) Add to this affirmation the beginnings of a friendship with Beat poet Allen Ginsberg, an acquaintance with the mad genius of jazz, Ornette Coleman, and the earth-shaking advent of the Beatles, and a different way of doing things emerges. Something's breaking through, and it could be that there's more than one way to transcend a genre, poke past a paradigm, and upset a subculture. What's a folk artist to do when the supposed folk establishment starts laying down what's "folk" and what isn't? Dylan's best biographer, Robert Shelton, suggests that these were the days when Dylan set out to become a mass-media poet.

I've Got My Bob Dylan Mask On

Kim Gordon of Sonic Youth once observed that live musical performance is a situation in which people will pay to watch other people believe in themselves. True enough, and I'll only add that the confidence we pay to see probably has something to do with our desire to be near freedom, real honesty, and the possibility of real community. We pay and hope. If Dylan was to deliver at New York's Philharmonic Hall on Halloween night in 1964, he'd have to take on the forces of fake authenticity without getting preachy and tell it like it is without becoming a caricature of himself. After opening with the recent songs his audience would expect concerning the shaky ethics of boxing and anticommunist paranoia, he introduces a new, stranger number, "Gates of Eden," as "A Sacrilegious Lullaby in D minor." The fragmented, more elusive quality of his recent liner notes has now made its way into the music (cowboy angels, utopian monks on the golden calf, and lampposts with folded arms). But the song is just a song, like the ones that came before, another way of fitting words together, another attempt at story. They've carefully taken in his carefully enunciated phrases, and he won't trouble them with an explanation, but he will make fun of the idea that he's just shared something inaccessibly deep, complex, or scary: "It's just Halloween. I've got my Bob Dylan mask on. . . . I'm mask-erading."

Skipping the gravitas, mocking it even, he moves swiftly on to the more obviously ridiculous "If You Gotta Go, Go Now." Like Andy Kaufman, he will claim no particular job description save that of a song-and-dance man, and the question of whether he's to be taken more or less seriously is something with which he won't concern himself. That's someone else's business. It's on to another new one they've never heard before: "It's All Right Ma, It's Life and Life Only" will appear on *Bringing It All Back Home* as "It's Alright Ma (I'm Only Bleeding)." The audience laughs at the title and he laughs in response, "Yes, it's a very funny song."

It isn't a funny song. While we can note that, for a "song-and-dance man," there is something amusing about the seven-minute "It's Alright Ma" on this particular evening, it is also the Dylan song that, possibly more than any other, would be regarded with the utmost seriousness. The song marks the day of judgment for every death-dealing abstraction, con game, and unjust ruler within view. Marshall McLuhan once observed that anyone who thinks there's a difference between education and entertainment doesn't know the first thing about either, and this song perhaps proves the point. One line that would be applauded for forty years of live performance through several administrations proclaims that even the U.S. president, some of these days, will have to stand naked. Money doesn't talk so much as it swears (a George Harrison favorite). And a line savored by Jimmy Carter lays down the truism that anyone not busy being born is busily dying. Lest we think our young entertainer is getting too high and mighty and moralistic, Dylan ends the invective with the confession that if the authorities could see his "thought-dreams," he'd likely be duly escorted to the guillotine. Not bad for a twenty-three-year-old.

Here's an alternative aesthetic for the liberal lynch mob. And anyone calling for the head of Oswald or Timothy McVeigh or John Walker Lindh is invited to have a long look at their own inner evil-doer; to see themselves in the outcast of the month. Like the Pharisee in Jesus' story, we're free to look down on the tax collector and thank God we're not as bad as *that,* but the slow train Dylan's talking about isn't easily boarded by people who deem some more equal (or worthy) than others. You don't get to deserve it. You don't get to exclude.

In recent years, when pressed concerning the meaning of a song, Dylan has noted, in mock exasperation, that nobody ever asked Elvis what he really meant when he sang about a hound dog. As frustrating as it might be for folk purists and professional intellectuals, he's determined to be a "pop" entertainer. And the notion that the entertainer (or artist or poet) need not explain, that it's even a little unseemly to expect an explanation, will be a tricky one to articulate for the "popular" artist. When Thom Yorke of Radiohead says that his lyrics are only gibberish or Jeff Tweedy of Wilco laughs at someone pronouncing him a prophet, they're using a public space cleared largely by Dylan, who could combine the political relevance of

Woody Guthrie and the popular appeal of Elvis Presley without losing himself completely. Social criticism as musical entertainment.
Poetry for the people. When the audience needed it, he knew how to
put his Bob Dylan mask on. In 1964, he began to create a media per-
sona he could knowingly mess with. Within a year or two, he'd be
telling his television audience, "Keep a good head and always carry
a lightbulb." He could be Charlie Chaplin *and* Walt Whitman *and*
Fats Waller. There was never a need to boundary it all up. There still
isn't. What could be more Americana than that?

And in another sense, he'd begun to learn the hard way that being
truthful (in metaphor or testimony) is the only way to bear witness,
and, for his part, the song means what the song means. When asked
to explain a particular song, Elvis Costello (an unashamed Dylan
devotee) observed that, if he could have put it another way, in a sentence for instance, he wouldn't have written the song. If he could have
said it in a sentence, he would have. Or in the case of Steve Earle, a
song about John Walker Lindh isn't, properly speaking, a statement
about John Walker Lindh. It's a song. It speaks for itself. "This Land
Was Made for You and Me" means, oddly enough, that this land was
made for you and me.

In the Halloween performance, an especially illuminating moment
occurs when someone in the audience, getting in the spirit of things,
asks for a cover of "Mary Had a Little Lamb." "God, did I write that?"
Dylan responds. " 'Mary Had a Little Lamb.' Is that a protest song?"
And in a fit of laughter, the audience is shown that they, too, can have
it more ways than one. It *can* matter. But nobody's going to try to
make it matter. That would be cheating. The either/or need not apply.
Without ambiguity, the jig is up. Anyone with an ear to hear will get
it. Call it "protest" or "nursery rhyme." Everyday is poetry. And
poetry is the thing that never ends.

Within months, "Subterranean Homesick Blues" (existential? sur-
real? nonsense? comedy?) would bust open expectations even further
(with ripples reaching everyone from R.E.M. to hip-hop to Nirvana
to Radiohead) and, in time, he would even "go electric" with what
Dylan would call "thin wild mercury music." He would wear dark
glasses (decades before Bono donned his *Achtung Baby*-era shades)
and arrive for an interview with a lightbulb, silently daring reporters

to ask him what it's for. A media blitz was simply another opportunity for a song-and-dance man to exhibit freedom and speak truth to the powerful and the people underneath. To name a few, John Lennon, Patti Smith, Richard Pryor, and Michael Stipe would do it too. But in 1964, Dylan walked this particular tightrope mostly alone.

Almost forty years later, *Love and Theft* would emerge with a seeming effortlessness from his Neverending (and still going) Tour. He tips his hat to Warren Zevon, Buddy Holly, and Charley Patton, noting that affectionate borrowing and standing on the shoulders of giants is all any of us can manage when we try to speak out loud; pure, absolute originality is a bit of a myth. But something of an amused acknowledgment of his place along the continuum of folk/protest/ punk/rock/entertainment might be coming through in "Summer Days" when he asks how we can honestly say we love someone else "when you know it's me all the time?" Surely an icon is allowed to wax self-referential from time to time. And as he doubtless understands (as he's testified, in fact), it's all a masquerade. There's actually a lot of that going around these days.

Ring Them Bells

"This is a *fictitious* story," Dylan once humorously noted concerning a song. Or even better, "*This* is taken out of the newspapers. And nothing has been changed except the words."[13] There are many ways, as Jeff Tweedy put it, to go about writing your mind the way you want it to read, trying to make sense of yourself to yourself, picturing a world gone wrong. In *City of Words*, Tony Tanner describes "a world of unprogrammed possibilities" that characterizes the creative impulse within much American creative expression.[14] And if we think again of the Silver Leaf Quartette of Norfolk's "Daniel Saw the Stone," there is always a more imaginative way to interpret the sounds and fury of the debilitating Babylonian present. The redeeming stone will unmake the oppressive blueprints we've been handed into better, clearer, truer stories, making them signify something. When Sly and the Family Stone tell us we shouldn't let "the plastic" get us down or Beck dreams up ways of feeling less alone in the "New Pollution," they're giving a name to domineering presences that, left unnamed, will possess the minds of millions. Rock 'n' roll will often resonate with the many ways the Bible laughs at our unacknowledged idolatries. When these bells are sounded in biblical history, the fire alarm of good news for the downtrodden and confused, they're very hard to unring.

The rolling stone not made by human hands has a way of bringing down the anxiety structures (Babel, Babylon) we've constructed in our fear and arrogance, mocking every manifestation of Ahab consciousness. This Jes Grew business will splinter into stranger forms, adapting itself to suit the times, unveiling all the new ways we've hypnotized ourselves into unawareness, boxing up our sympathies to better suit our comfort levels.

When Kris Kristofferson sings in his low, gruff voice about the wide assortment ("funky bunch of friends") that Jesus gathers about himself in "Jesus Was a Capricorn," deriding the way that everybody craves somebody else to look down on, someone to feel better than, we can receive the good word that our fastidiousness (the easy habit of finding others hopelessly offensive) is of the Devil. We seem to have a knack, Kristofferson intones, of hating anything we don't understand. "The Law Is for the Protection of the People" testifies to the crucifying impulse of self-described "decent folks" who don't want "riddle-speaking prophets" disturbing the peace which is no peace. This is music for the country by the country.

To think beyond programmed prejudice and delay the rush to judgment (as a hipster or a square) is the beginning of wisdom. When we're made to listen to catchy, disarming portrayals of someone else's joys and sorrows (from *Goodbye, Babylon* to Vic Chesnutt), we're enabled to think more clearly and kindly about other people. A thriving democracy requires this sort of equipment. And if we think of democratic dignity as primarily the property of National Public Radio or a "religious thing" or an annoying attempt to be "politically correct," we're in big trouble. We're trapped inside our suspicious minds.

To be people of amazing grace is to see ourselves as recipients of unowed kindness and understanding, and if we really believe it's been lavished upon us undeservedly, maybe we can lavish a little upon the people we find ourselves least inclined to view generously. If we're showering only the people we *already* love with love, do we really think grace is all that amazing? Are we any different from anyone else in our behavior? Do we really believe in amazing grace at all? Or have we placed a limit on it, somehow expecting it to abide by our national and cultural boundaries?

The amused affection of the Jes Grew impulse won't let us kid ourselves about our own ungraciousness or the common life of our multiple pilgrim species. I suspect we're often drawn to live musical performance in an attempt to somehow get in the mood of this ancient solidarity of silliness, something to enliven the daily grind. We want the company of mysterious tramps who know what it's like to feel strange, who seem unafraid to testify about feeling down and unwanted, who can sing a word of rebuke to our inner Ahabs.

On the Pixies album *Doolittle*, Frank Black (masquerading as Black Francis) begins a song called "Mr. Grieves" with a kind of reggae riff and the repeated hope that everything is going to be all right. As he makes this proclamation, he starts to laugh in a not-so-convincing manner, and as he tries again, the laughter becomes a sort of angry, barely controlled sobbing, and we know that everything isn't going to be all right. It's completely silly, of course. And it is, technically, only a performance, but it's deeply liberating to hear Frank Black play out a scene of lost composure, satirizing it by acknowledging it, letting a little air in. It almost hurts to hear it, but it's funny because it's true, and the recognition of severe dysfunction (Psalms, Shakespeare, Violent Femmes) can alleviate the pain. It brings it out into the open—songs of love and loss and nervous breakdown. We should be wary of being overly offended by comedic lamentation or poignant portrayals of screwed-uppedness. If we feel completely unsympathetic toward the silliness, it might be that we aren't sufficiently offended by ourselves.

Pixies enthusiasts have signed on for this brand of communication, recognizing themselves in the songs and the tensions to which they testify. Frank Black will cop a wide variety of attitudes to suit the neuroses of different songs. This is how the music works. It's an entering into a communal awareness, a partaking of the mother wit that resists the despair with nothing to say. If "punk" might be defined as a commitment to question everything, it, too, exists in the wake of the ancient rolling stone. There are a variety of countertactics to be pieced together in song and story against dehumanization on behalf of all things human, and we might not get it the first time around. We're welcome to be troubled by something we're shown by Tori Amos, Trent Reznor, or Randy Newman, but if we're refusing the testimony of the truthful word, the witness, or the confession, we risk losing the ability to hear or love well at all. Only truthfulness can edify. And finding any and everything interesting and worthy of song is a habit of the long, practiced, determined wit of Jes Grew, dethroning the mighty and chanting down Babylon at every opportunity and in all of its multiplying forms.

John Prine's "Your Flag Decal Won't Get You into Heaven Anymore" names an amusing cultural paradox that hardly requires explanation. It's not knocking flag decals exactly, but it does name a confused association rather aptly, juxtaposing the Sermon on the Mount with "My country right or wrong." And as we're inundated with all kinds of antiwisdom, glorified, superficial beauty and unexamined thinking, we need sanity-restoring ways of looking at it all. We need finer work songs to better keep out the chill. Songs that might possibly serve as a moral compass as we look over the maps, legends, and blueprints we've inherited and all the rage and irritability that proffer themselves as tradition.

Welcome to the Occupation

And with this, it should be obvious that we're back in Cherrycoke territory, an underground ethos of good-humored resistance that speaks back to everyday chaos, songs and sounds that somehow describe what we're going through. Prine's "Angel from Montgomery" gives powerful expression to a woman who pines for a word, any word, from a husband who won't even tell her about his workday as her hopes and dreams for a loving future diminish. A familiar story-turned-prayer. In R.E.M.'s "New Test Leper," Michael Stipe puts the words of Jesus on the lips of an embarrassed guest on a television sideshow. It comes out awkwardly, but he'd hoped to illuminate the minds of the audience in the studio and the people at home with the dictum of "Judge not; lest ye be judged." As we would expect, this doesn't go over well, and he's made to sit silent as he's cut off by commercials and the host's "index-carded" wit. Identifying with the postmodern leper, Stipe reminds us of the life outside the conventionally telegenic, whose aching smiles feel too unattractive to look upon. That would be most of us.

The music of democratic dignity is possessed by an ethos of everyone invited and every testimony worthy of a kind, interested, sympathetic ear. It's scandalously open to the notion that anybody anywhere might have a worthwhile vision. It trusts that a revelatory word can come from the least among us at anytime, that those we're least likely to want to listen to might have one. The music assumes that there is no human life unworthy of our affectionate interest. And I don't think it too far-fetched to suggest that a young Bob Dylan bore faithful witness to this folk culture, of and for the people, when he voiced a word of insistent empathy for Lee Harvey Oswald in 1963. A moment's reflection might bring to mind a number of examples of this sort of thing in Dylan's catalog (Hattie Carroll, "Hurricane" Carter), Springsteen's invocation of working-class heroes and the ghost of Tom Joad, or Pearl Jam ("Jeremy," "Daughter," "Better Man"). But for my money, the career of R.E.M., hailing from the local culture of Athens, Georgia, is especially noteworthy for self-consciously democratic, resiliently compassionate music that spans decades as it speaks for, to, and despite the times.

In 1986, *Lifes Rich Pageant* opens with a call to heed the insurgency that was and is America ("Begin the Begin"), and the summons to look harder in the eyes of our neighbors and consider again the histories we've inherited is indicative of their entire catalog. With an eye fixed on all that might make American culture redemptively unique in the history of nations, R.E.M. rages against the machinery that will always feel threatened by an unconditional affirmation of all human beings as infinitely worthwhile. This is perhaps especially evident on "Exhuming McCarthy," which laments the loss of a sense of decency in public discourse as the general welfare is sold off to the highest bidder. According authorial authority to a disabled child ("Wrong Child"), Montgomery Clift ("Monty Got a Raw Deal"), an out-of-work Confederate soldier ("Swan Swan H"), and a confused, angry television viewer who saw fit to physically attack CBS News anchor

Dan Rather ("What's the Frequency, Kenneth?"), their music documents the viewpoints of various unheeded, marginalized voices.

While "Everybody Hurts" off *Automatic for the People* (1992) is
probably their best-known ballad thus far (a finer anthem for the democratic solidarity of all things human is hard to come by), my personal
favorite is their deeply uplifting recording of "Try Not to Breathe." As
legend has it, the phrase of the title was stumbled upon in the recording studio when Stipe was instructed to maintain silence behind the
microphone. "I'll try not to breathe," developed into the musings of a
citizen of advanced age who doesn't want to burden the young with
too much in the way of caregiving or worry while nevertheless entertaining the hope that someone somewhere down the line might want
to listen to some stories. The citizen wants someone to remember his
or her testimony. An odd accomplishment for what we usually expect
in a pop song, admittedly, but "Try Not to Breathe" challenges the listener to look more generously and believe more widely and richly concerning the value of a stranger. They've seen things we'll never see.
The stranger will often be a warehouse of wisdom and stories, an endless supply of human interest only so long as humans go to the blessed
trouble of finding one another interesting. Remembering each other
and paying attention is what we get to do. It's of and for the people.
Wouldn't it be something if we did it automatically? Might we make
it a habit? Might we learn that trustworthy witness will usually come
from unexpected quarters? There's something very R.E.M. about this
sensibility. Very folksy. The student of Waffle House politics has a
long-practiced understanding of the stranger as an occasion for joy.
And a nation of diasporas gets to be especially adept at listening to one
another. The children of immigrants will often have particular affection for every kind of redemption song.

R.E.M. concern themselves with the kind of people we find in
country songs, hip-hop, daytime television, and Charles Bukowski
poems. The music risks all on redemptive possibilities and all these
oddly resurrectable human beings. It assumes that we're not yet
young, that there's always a better way of putting things, and that
there's no telling when someone might do a Lazarus in the land of Jes
Grew. This redemptively curious attitude is captured particularly well
in the band's fascination with Andy Kaufman ("Man on the Moon"

and "The Great Beyond") who could make the outrageous appear doubly ridiculous by portraying it as it is in the world of Wrestlemania or any and all entertainment media. When Stipe imitates Kaufman imitating Elvis Presley, we're made to think about celebrity, nostalgia, and public performance very differently. Popular entertainment is demystified long enough to be beheld in all its strangeness as a mode of social interaction. Our mean ideas can have us feeling pretty psyched at concerts, political rallies, and wrestling matches, but we're all just humans: Dylan and Presley and Oswald alike. We need something to help us remember as much, something to keep us thinking kindly and carefully. If we believe there's something worthy of song up every stranger's sleeve, then maybe everyone's cool.

American music will articulate the otherwise unarticulated testaments of troubled souls ("great" and "small") in troubled times. Johnny Cash's "The Ballad of Ira Hayes" describes the drunken death of a Native American soldier who helped raise the flag at Iwo Jima and returned to a racist homeland. Beck's "All in Your Mind" describes the dismay of gradually discovering a dear friend has gone scared stiff and demon possessed. And Tom Waits gives voice to countless castoffs, respectability long lost, who note in Orbisonesque fashion that you're "Innocent When You Dream." We're all more than a little human, and there's nothing especially simple or straightforward about humans. Folk music always says so.

When Dylan speaks of first hearing Woody Guthrie ("Last Thoughts on Woody Guthrie") or Michael Stipe recalls hearing Patti Smith ("E-Bow the Letter"), we're reminded of how democratic solidarity makes its way through the masses. They're offering personal testimony concerning the work of cultural appropriation that, in the long run, might begin to name how we get from Jesus' career in the Middle East to Tom Waits's howl of new day on the way. They're describing the moment they happened upon an undercurrent of liveliness and sociability that they felt compelled to seek out and make their own. Better ways of being free and speaking truthfully to and about the world invigorate the listener, putting words, expressions, and images to an otherwise mostly undescribed existence. People need to know that they're not alone in their awkwardness as they struggle to find their skin. They want to hear their own hopes and dreams interpreted in new, truer fashions. And the truer fashions will build redemptively on the old ones. Not better stories than their own, but explanations more dignifying and liberating than the prisons and paradigms in which they find themselves. Prayers and songs that cover everything, even the sadness that seems to defy sense and all the strangeness that doesn't seem to bother anyone else. A music of the misfits, by the misfits, for the misfits. For anyone who's felt this way. The authorial authority of the People's Republic of Rock 'n' Roll. The good news according to anyone called out of Egyptian hard times.

Listen Here

In Robert Altman's *Buffalo Bill and the Indians, or Sitting Bull's History Lesson,* putting on history (enacting or performing it) is the big business with which Paul Newman's Buffalo Bill hopes to corner the entertainment market. Sending out his research assistant for more stories and personalities to cast into his live "re-enactments," he wants to make sure everyone under him remembers one guideline: "Anything historical is mine." To which comes the dutiful reply: "Everything historical is yours, Bill." As they're rehearsing for a production, one of Bill's men remarks, "We're in the authentic business." And of course, when Sitting Bull himself is brought in to participate, he will have some very unique and authoritative views concerning authenticity and history ("History is nothing but disrespect for the dead").

In discussions on the subject of American popular music, the question of authenticity is usually somewhere nearby. It isn't necessarily reflected in record sales, but it's always somewhere behind the talk. Who can claim authenticity? Who's really doing it? Who's in the Jordan? Who's standing in there with the Carter Family and Carl Perkins and James Brown? Who really means it?

The idea of authenticity sells Levi's even when they aren't made in America anymore, and a successful invocation of Johnny Cash or Billy Graham can probably win an election. But being in "the authentic business" is clearly a contradiction. History won't be bought or sold or co-opted. Like Jes Grew, it's scandalously multipartisan, with an eye on more parties than the human mind can hold. It can absorb within itself more viewpoints than a Republican National Convention, but it won't be owned by anyone. Too knowing an explanation of what history meant, as if we own it and know it better than the dead who lived it, makes history a solved problem over which we need no longer scratch our heads and by which we're no longer haunted. But as William Faulkner tells it, "The past is never dead. It's not even past."[15] It's a living presence in which we live and move and have our being, and putting too fine a point on what it was "all about" or what it "just goes to show" is indeed, to put the matter mildly, a form of unthinking, character-assassinating disrespect. Sitting Bull was right.

Any language that presumes proprietorship over the authentic, the free, the godly, or the truthful is a bearing of false witness, and I don't believe we can entertain such language for long without going off the rails. As I understand it, good music summons us to revere ourselves, the people nearby, and the history we're standing in with a bit more tenderness, awe, and amusement. It also inspires an imaginative vigilance, dislocating the fixations that keep us thinking and speaking falsely; a vigilance that anything approaching emotional health thrives on. With a close regard for history and what's going on in the world, the songs are written by and for people who want to have a go at not becoming psychopaths. We write psalms and songs to keep from going crazy and to make sense of the senseless. We listen, watch, and pray as a form of crazy-prevention. We're not alone.

When we talk about the music or any history of faithful witness or truthful testimony, nobody gets to be an absolute authority, an expert, or a theologian who can see undarkly. No nation, culture, or political party can claim to speak definitively for freedom itself. Who claims complete, undivided truthfulness, truth abandons. And there is no professional opinion on the human soul. But we can aspire to be true to the songs of lone pilgrims, apostles, poor immigrants, and escaped slaves. We do well to be haunted by them, and we can hope that our own words won't sound hopelessly untrue, unwise, or dishonest beside them. All we can do is hope.

One song that traces a particular pathway of Jes Grew (from Jerusalem to New Orleans) and the myriad ways our ancestors published salvation and lamentation abroad is Dylan's "Blind Willie McTell." As something of an aspiring bluesman himself, Dylan imagines that being worthy of the Word of God, the blues, or the stories and songs of the past is a non-option, but bearing stuttering witness might be a possibility. We might at least pay attention. One can try to tune in well and be an echo among other echoes, more or less faithful, in a landscape of power and greed and seemingly endless defensiveness. We get to add to the heaping collection of testimonials and eyewitness accounts of weird goings-on and broken dreams. And a good song might at least point someone further back, urging them to look a little harder for better songs and forgotten voices in the deep chrome canyons of multiplying Manhattans where people find it hard to remember or listen to much of anything. One good word might turn us on to a lively Jes Grew culture going on beneath the radar of most executives and profiteers.

God's Money

The language that notes the steady hegemony of chrome canyons and worry over gone and forgotten soulishness is borrowed from a persistent sensibility in Wilco's *A Ghost Is Born* (2004), an album, like many others, I'd like to see packaged up next to *Goodbye, Babylon.* In a song like "Hell Is Chrome," Jeff Tweedy submits for our approval the notion that hell might sometimes sell itself with a sense of belonging and proprietary happiness, a collective sense of *us*, readily available to be pitted against *them*. Like evil, hell has long been too clever to present itself as bad news for self-respecting decent folks, and the Devil gave up red some time ago. As Blind Willie Johnson or Sister O. M. Terrell would remind us, there's a certain broad path that leads to destruction, so we probably shouldn't feel at home in every atmosphere that calls itself homey or every party that advertises itself as united, saturated in wholesome values, and tough on other people's terror. A winning attitude is readily available in exchange for a little soul, but really coming clean, in "Spiders (Kidsmoke)," won't even be a possibility until we learn to say what we mean. Never an easy prospect for poor, American sinners, but surely a worthwhile sentiment for a nation under God.

The thinning down of hearts and minds and the professional, religious experts who murder to dissect are powerfully addressed in

"Theologians." With a liberal borrowing from John's Gospel, Tweedy hauls out Jesus' cryptic talk of laying down his life to better hasten the arrival of the Holy Spirit. In what might serve as a brilliantly nuanced take on John's gospel account, Jesus throws himself into the death-dealing mechanism of stupidity, corruption, and mob violence, lets it do its worst, and there's been a ghost in the machinery ever since. Nothing will be the same from now on. Century upon century, waking from a stony sleep, we're haunted by a Christ who single-handedly brought up the net value of human beings for every culture that takes him seriously. Lynching will occasionally fall out of favor. All manner of things made new. Everyone counts. There's a Pentecost going on, but you won't often hear it on the radio.

As a possible companion piece to "Blind Willie McTell," *A Ghost Is Born* ends with "The Late Greats," a song that pays homage to the unacknowledged, unnoticed, unsigned, systematically underestimated poetry that people like Tweedy, Dylan, and numberless legions of collectors will champion whenever they're privileged enough to unearth it. It's so good (the Late Great's "Turpentine") that you can never know it. It's never even been recorded. Too magic to hold. Too holy to achieve much in the way of mass appeal. You can't sell a covenant. Like the rolling stone that raises people from the dead, all we can do is try and bear witness to it and sing in recollection and expectation of its promise. The table is spread.

But in all of Wilco's longing for a "Bible-black predawn" and their songs on the necessity of learning how to die, I'd have to present the Jes Grew award to "Jesus, etc." off *Yankee Hotel Foxtrot*. In a sentiment as powerful as anything I've heard in popular music, Tweedy ties all smug abstraction to the living earth when he suggests that determined love, active in the world, might best be understood as the sum total of God's money. It moves, as Dante put it, the sun and the other stars. It's how the divine economy goes. As a radically incarnate ethos for life and how to live it, the suggestion sits well alongside some other ones occasionally heard on the radio: Love is all we need. God *is* love. The one who loves is of God. It's been the only way to effectively war on war ever since Jesus threw everything off balance. A risky proposition, like having to lose your life to find it, but for cosmic, earthbound gospel, it's hard to beat. Rock on. Sweetness follows.

Chapter 5

The Signposts Up Ahead:
Taking Our Own Temperature

So at the dinner table when I was very young, I was boring to all those other people. They did not want to hear about the dumb childish news of my days. They wanted to talk about really important stuff that happened in high school or maybe in college or at work. So the only way I could get into a conversation was to say something funny. I think I must have done it accidentally at first, just accidentally made a pun that stopped the conversation. . . . And then I found that a joke was a way to break into an adult conversation.
                                                    —*Kurt Vonnegut*

There is more than one way to burn a book.
                                                    —*Ray Bradbury*

What helps for me—if help comes at all—is to find the mustard seed of the funny at the core of the horrible and futile.
                                                    —*Philip K. Dick*

The Universe is not only stranger than we imagine; it is stranger than we can *imagine.*
                                                    —*J. B. S. Haldane*

*I*f we carefully imagine a young Kurt Vonnegut sitting at a busy, chattering dinner table wondering how he might get in on the fun, we might help ourselves out of the defense mechanism that makes poetry, Faulkner novels, and Bob Dylan into weird, inaccessible, unnecessarily convoluted offerings. Vonnegut (like the rest of us)

wants in. A way of relating, some excuse to be heard, an attention get-
ter that will serve to incorporate his perspective into the conversation.
How to do this? How might we get someone to say, "That's interesting! I never thought of it that way," and look at us with an appreciative smile? How might we achieve the attentiveness of our fellow
creatures at the Waffle House?

With "The Fire Balloons" (1951), Ray Bradbury offers a "Once
Upon A Time . . ." featuring a couple of Episcopalian ministers trying to share Jesus with "the Old Ones" of Mars. How's this going
to work? An interesting thought experiment, to say the least, and it
can get the mind wondering about a lot of other things as well. And
as the Reverend Cherrycoke might remind us, such confabulation
isn't *merely* a story, in the dismissive sense; rather, it's a way of
describing the present world (the stranger and livelier the better) to
a world in danger of being disenchanted with itself. It's not a pre-
diction so much as a way of talking about what's going on, a
reminder that we're free to think about things differently now.
Orwell's *1984* isn't rendered irrelevant by the fact that we aren't
divided into Oceania and Eurasia at the minute. Doublethink, Reality Control, and Thoughtcrime describe lived experience. And
Slaughter-House Five (chronicling Billy Pilgrim's relationship
with his green friends on Trafamadore and his prescription of corrective lenses for Earthling souls) is one way Vonnegut can try to
bear witness to his experience as soldier and the destruction of
Dresden in World War II. And so it goes.

When we first begin to write songs and poems and science fiction,
we begin with the hope that we might have something to say, but it
isn't as if the stories are simply vehicles for morals or messages. As
thought experiments, Wilco's *Yankee Hotel Foxtrot* and R.E.M.'s
Automatic for the People give us a lot to think about on the subjects
of success, power, and God's money, but, as Flannery O'Connor
points out, it isn't as if one should start with an abstraction and then
come up with a story or a "concept album" to house the thing. If
what's being said could be said nonmetaphorically, we should probably give it a try. Otherwise, the proffered "art" might best be understood as propaganda. The good story works differently. It tells the
truth and tells it strange.

Peace Offensive

Around the time of the Korean War, film producer Julien Blaustein became preoccupied by the paradoxical phrase appearing in news headlines and spoken by self-respecting world leaders everywhere: "Peace Offensive." Looking for a story to speak to the tension, he eventually found the piece (Harry Bates's "Farewell to the Master") that became *The Day the Earth Stood Still.* And from the intergalactic calm and moral authority of Michael Rennie's Klaatu to the stalwart grandeur of Gort, this word on worldly ambition stands rather well. The publicity that preceded its release in 1951 (WHAT IS THIS INVADER FROM ANOTHER PLANET . . . CAN IT DESTROY THE EARTH?) plays to the very paranoia that the film mocks and derides, and the film's success (like that of the Beats and Ray Bradbury) suggests that the American public was eager for a perspective-enlarging word.

It is only after the American military shoots and wounds the newly arrived Klaatu ("We have come to visit you in peace and with goodwill") within seconds of his landing in Washington that the enormous robot Gort slowly exits the spaceship and begins to obliterate tanks and cannons and machine guns with a laser located behind his head visor. Blaustein once recounted that, in a preview screening, he was horrified to note that audiences laughed at the first sight of Gort. But in time, he realized that they weren't amused by Gort so much as the presumption on the part of anyone "in power" that this impasse had a military solution or that the arrival of an extraterrestrial required an adversarial posture to begin with. When a radio announcer solemnly proclaims, "We are dealing with forces beyond our knowledge and power," and the president reluctantly concedes, "We may be up against powers that are beyond our control," the science fiction genre once again creates a space for an acknowledgement of our limits and our less telegenic and (for some) less confidence-inspiring finiteness; wars on terror and efforts to rid the world of evil not withstanding.

Like C. S. Lewis's *Out of the Silent Planet* and Ursula K. Le Guin's Ekumen series, *The Day the Earth Stood Still* offers the possibility of a larger ethical order within which our sense of polity and profit will have to reorient itself, and, in this sense, science fiction can serve as a mode of apocalypse. When Lewis identifies Earth as the silent, rebel planet that has yet to get in line with the greater cosmos, more in sync with God's shalom, we're invited to think again about our have-to's, our evildoers, and our less redemptive passions. Similarly, Le Guin's Ekumen (a sort of democratic, intergalactic Vatican) won't presume to define freedom for the rest of the universe ("from the top down," as it were), but her descriptions can get the imagination working and expanding beyond the "Washington Consensus" and the suggestion that history (written by the winners, after all) is nothing more than the memory of states. The tendency toward messianic uppityness and overweening faith in our ability to easily perceive and do the right thing is tempered by these moral visions. Klaatu brings tiding of peacefulness and words of admonition concerning Earth's escalating aggression. Even if all sides inevitably term themselves "peacekeepers and freedom-fighters," Klaatu assures them that, however they might choose to name their evil, any spread of their hostilities will earn the wrath of Gort.

The president sends a secretary to meet with Klaatu in a closed room, and he tries to articulate the homeland security concerns that might not always coincide with Klaatu's desire to take his gospel to all of Earth's nations. Klaatu wants the president to try and think of him as a neighbor, but the secretary explains that it's difficult for his fellow Earthlings to think of Klaatu as a neighbor; true neighborliness between anyone being a rather delicate matter. "I'm afraid in the present situation you'll have to learn to think that way," Klaatu replies. He will take his errand of mercy outside of the nation's security apparatus and travel under the name of "Carpenter" (Get it?). And if the moral arc of the universe bends toward justice, his word will eventually find allegiance on Earth as it already is in the heavens.

Strange Neurosis

With Gort alongside, the image of Klaatu wishing us well and looking compassionately but knowingly at our hysteria is an enduring one. It's indicative of the interest in human moral progress (and recidivism) at work throughout classic science fiction. To be able to laugh at the human foibles made manifest in our suspicious dimwit-tedness before the unknown is to enter into a kind of ecumenical laughter that privileges no party or tribe (a little like the indiscrimi-nate satire available on *The Simpsons*). And yet there's also a less amused, antitotalitarian impulse pervading these thought experi-ments; a hypersensitivity for the more elusive forces of unfreedom.

Philip K. Dick had a powerful aversion for anything that seemed to justify the reduction of human beings to their "use" value. View-ing people (or training them to view themselves) as machines exist-ing for someone else's purposes struck him as being "the greatest evil imaginable."[1] And resisting "pseudohuman behavior" or "inauthen-tic human activity" struck him as the most pressing need in our soci-ety.[2] Borrowing Tom Paine's complaint about Europe, "They admired the feathers and forgot the bird," Dick remarked, "It is the dying bird that I am concerned with. The dying—and yet, I think, beginning again to revive in the hearts of the new generation of kids coming into maturity—the dying bird of authentic humanness."[3] The fear that the inhumane has come to pass as standard procedure or a basic requirement for living in "the real world" is a recurring theme throughout American science fiction.

One of the early classics dealing with communal dehumanization is *Invasion of the Body Snatchers* (1956). Describing the plight of Kevin McCarthy's Dr. Miles J. Bennell, the preview declares, "AN ACCURSED, DREADFUL, MALEVOLENT THING WAS HAP-PENING TO THOSE HE LOVED." His patients come to see him in droves, complaining that their loved ones aren't themselves, that they've been replaced by impersonators. But gradually, fewer people are complaining, and most apologize for having been so unreason-able. His psychologist friend, Danny Kauffman, explains it as "a strange neurosis . . . evidently contagious—an epidemic of mass hys-teria. In two weeks, it's spread all over town."

"What causes it?" Miles wonders.

"Worry about what's going on in the world probably."

But Kauffman, as it turns out, is one of *them*. It's the pods. While the citizens sleep, the pods absorb their minds and memories, grow into exact replicas, dispose of their bodies, and assume their identi-ties. Learning to stop worrying about the world means being replaced with a soulless counterpart with no affections, passions, or fanciful notions. Blissful sameness rules. "You're reborn into an untroubled world," the pod people assure Miles and his girlfriend, Becky Driscoll ("I felt something was wrong, but I thought it was me").

Against the commonsensical notion that too much concern over what's going on in the world is unseemly and mildly neurotic, there's a sensibility here that suggests we should be worried if we *aren't* unsettled every so often. Concern over rising health care costs or education funding isn't the sole province of economic girlie men, and distinguishing between different kinds of Muslims in the Arab world and seeking their testimony isn't anti-American. A nation that flees any and all unsettledness is a nation that wants to be brainwashed. If we resent troubling news that fails to verify our lifestyles, learning to reflexively improvise it away with the "liberal/conservative" bias or "anti-American" card, we're narrowing the zone in which we can see, think clearly, or confess wrongdoing. When we fail in the obligation to be vigilant against our own worst instincts, we find we're pleased (comforted even) to enter the neuroses of the herd.

Humans from Earth

When Karl Barth spoke of the strange, new world of the Bible, he was noting the manner in which the Bible undoes the reigning takes on reality, undermining our tendency to paint the world in our vanity's favor *and* speaking a particular kind of earth-bound, kingdom-coming hope to our anxiety-stricken landscape. When the Bible's made perfectly normal or obvious to anyone who shares our perfectly natural status quo values, we might do well to suspect we're in the presence of false witness. The word of God has an annoying way of unsettling our sense of what's fair and balanced. When read properly, it resists the tidying-up mechanism that Flannery O'Connor viewed with such disapproval. It frees us up to view ourselves strangely again.

As a youth, I was taught to read the Bible as if my life depended on it, but what I felt to be the intensity of its witness was only rarely reflected in the words and sensibilities of those whom Hawthorne describes with some degree of bemusement as professional teachers of truth. To my young mind, the supposed authorities never struck me as being sufficiently freaked out by the escalating stakes involved in the endless varieties of human screwiness at work in the world. And then came science fiction. I'd felt that something was wrong, and without these stories and images (my Woody Guthrie *and* my Patti Smith, if you will), I was at risk of assuming I was the only one. Enter Rod Serling.

With his odd and chronically underestimated witness, Serling insisted on viewing television as a medium of broad, sociological possibilities. In the fifties, his writing for *Kraft Television Theater* and *Playhouse 90* had earned him a living, but teleplays that spoke directly and unambiguously to such events as the murder of Emmett Till had just about put him out of a job. But he still maintained that television was potentially a mother lode of storytelling, consciousness-expanding, artistic expression. With *The Twilight Zone*, Serling would keep the airwaves weird and wonderful while noting how effectively words that couldn't be uttered by a Republican or a Democrat could be said loud and clear by a Martian. He would stand in front of the camera and narrate us through the weirdness of the world we're living in. As something of an anti-fascist crusader, Serling was unwilling to leave the biggest game in town, television (the drug of the nation), to soap and aspirin companies.

As a moral tale that lingers in the imagination, one of the most famous episodes, running a close second behind "To Serve Man," is "The Monsters Are Due on Maple Street." There is a power failure in the suburbs. For the denizens of Maple Street, the absence of evidence is not the evidence of absence, and the loss of electric power combined with some heresay concerning out-of-the-ordinary behavior among freedom-loving people will lead to every-man-for-himself, murderous mayhem. In their desire to root out the evil they suspect in one another while noting nothing threatening in their own hearts, they will destroy each other in the name of safety. Above the fray, one invading alien remarks to his apprentice that they've long learned that the most effective weapon of mass destruction is the random manipulation of electricity in one community at a time, whereby they conquer those who are more than willing to conquer themselves. (Serling's final thought: "The pity of it is that these things cannot be confined to the Twilight Zone.")

Serling was haunted by our disinclination to imagine the motivations, the mind-set, or the hopes of whoever it is we regard, from one year to the next, as our adversary. "A Quality of Mercy" features a Lieutenant Katell (played by Dean Stockwell of *Quantum Leap* fame) whose eagerness to lead an assault on some starved Japanese soldiers holed up in a cave on the Philippine Islands (1945) is suddenly put in a different light when he's inexplicably transformed into Lieutenant Yamuri, a Japanese officer contemplating an assault on wounded Americans on Corregidor (1942). As he pleads with his superior to forego an attack, he finds himself back on the Philippine Islands, driven by newer, larger motives than that which had seized him previously. Serling ends the episode extolling a wisdom (in this case borrowed from Shakespeare) applicable to all nations at all times.

Thought Lives

But my favorite *Twilight Zone* casts Burgess Meredith, a librarian on trial in a totalitarian state for the crime of "obsolescence," with Fritz Weaver's Chancellor presiding, in an episode titled "The Obsolete Man." In a fine characterization of the genre, Serling explains, "This is not a new world, it is simply an extension of what began in the old one. . . . It has refinements, technological advances, and a more sophisticated approach to the destruction of human freedom." Logic that fails to buttress the will to power is an enemy, and voices that don't coincide with the stratagems of that power (echoing an occasional characterization of the United Nations) are dismissed as irrelevant. As the Chancellor explains, "You're a bug, Mr. Wordsworth! A crawling insect. An ugly, misformed creature who has no purpose here, no meaning."

"I am a human being!" Wordsworth retorts against the judgment of the state with that authority of Earth-inheriting meekness characteristic of Burgess Meredith.

And after being assured that his "meaningless words" are without substance or dimension, weight or meaning, as they are out of tune with the state (less than nothing, according to the Chancellor), Wordsworth declares, "I don't care. I tell you I don't care. I'm a human being. I exist! And if I speak one thought aloud, that thought lives! Even after I'm shoveled into my grave."

The execution will be televised. And in a McLuhanesque observation, the Chancellor remarks, "It's not unusual that we televise executions; it has an educative effect on the population." But Wordsworth has an idea in mind for his televised, final moments, and it will involve an engagement with the principalities and powers of this present darkness. After Wordsworth stages a demythologizing epiphany for the Chancellor and the viewing public, Serling has a word on the state of the State that all, save Wordsworth, worshiped: "Any state, any entity, any ideology that fails to recognize the worth, the dignity, the rights of man, that state is obsolete. A case to be filed under 'M' for mankind . . . in the Twilight Zone."

Martin Luther King Jr. espoused a politics that viewed every human being as a soul of infinite metaphysical value. And as a word-fraught species, our politics will never be separated from the way we talk about each other, the words we use and the stories we tell to explain and justify our policies, decisions, and lifestyles. In a lifelong study of human behavior and the actions that are now and then described as "war crimes" (from My Lai to Abu Ghraib), Robert Jay Lifton developed the term "atrocity-producing situation" in an effort to name the way words speak actions into being and the way stories about absolute good and absolute evil can create the conditions (the scripts if you like) for confusion and gray areas over the very good and evil supposedly at stake, with generally well-meaning people playing maniacal roles that radically differ from the heroic self-conception they've been given as a blueprint.

Serling doesn't name nation-states in his narration, but I can imagine he would note a certain degree of Orwellian applicability in the assessment of a recent bipartisan Senate Intelligence Committee concerning intelligence failures: "groupthink." Their report, endorsed by all nine of the Republicans and eight Democrats on the committee, pins this atrocity-producing thought habit on the Central Intelligence

Agency without going so far as to suggest that war-making words on the part of any policymakers contributed to the hegemony of the herd instinct. Hostility toward honest questions and rejection of advice that doesn't coincide with our already-made-up minds will often call itself patriotism while sneering at any insight that seems too sensitive or nuanced. Any question concerning our sense of moral purity, irrepressible altruism, and love for all of humankind can be shot down as anti-American. But the whistle-blower is the real patriot when groupthink has almost silenced all hope of redemptive opposition. Wordsworth will give everything for his culture as a minority of one. Is his public still capable of being moved? Are we?

The tale of Romney Wordsworth's assertion of the sacred power of one human voice against the secular fundamentalism of the state is one of those stories (like Melville's, Hawthorne's, Dylan's) in which the language of redemptive violence loses its emotional appeal and is deprived of its credibility. It moves in the flow of the moral continuum that this book hopes to identify and celebrate, a movement of truthfulness making people free. The memory of the story (Wordsworth vs. State) can serve as a reference in our ethical dilemmas (required viewing for public service?) and a source of illumination concerning our tendency to find peacefulness offensive when we're in the grip of the power of pride.

In the wide world of sports, brand names, wrestling, and presidential campaigns, we won't usually go broke selling a sense of belonging. But just because we can sell T-shirts and bumper stickers and win elections with a sense of outrage doesn't mean we have to give in to its tactics. When America's public discourse is reduced to two parties trying to outshout each other concerning how angry they are about other people's evil, the mantras inevitably work their way into our conversations with spouses, neighbors, brothers, and sisters. We need a Romney Wordsworth who reminds us that we live our lives under the gaze of a just God who knows our innermost thoughts as if we were shouting them, who opposes the proud but gives grace to the humble, and who notices our hateful words even after we've learned to surround ourselves with people who talk the same way. It will cost him his life, but Wordsworth will offer the demystifying, prophetic word. It's always costly.

The Word Is Fancy

The realization that we are all the time seeing and speaking in a state of moral myopia, all too often equipped with blinders that obstruct the possibility of wider visions, can be a liberating one. Serling isn't a pessimist or a cynic but a hopeful realist. Living up to the moral breakthroughs of history requires a determination never to rest from trying to break through further. A community that operates under the mostly unspoken assumption that we've somehow reached a plateau (or that, as a famous beer commercial puts it, "It don't get no better than this") shouldn't be characterized as optimistic, positive, or morally uplifting. From the perspective of the sci-fi sensibility, that would mean that the pods have won, and the status quo is the carefully defined sanity of wordless despair and plastic smiles.

The alternative mind-set present throughout much science fiction is one of Always Further To Go, endless frontiers, and strange, new ways of describing a creation whose strangeness knows no end. As Philip K. Dick insisted, "Joy is the essential and final ingredient of science fiction, the joy of discovery of newness."[4] And the discoveries invite us to forget our defensively held views long enough to sympathize with other people and possibilities that aren't as comforting or familiar as we might prefer. But without these discoveries, we can't learn, forgive, or be born into anything we aren't already. We can't develop or change our already made-up minds.

In Dick's *The Man In The High Castle* (1962), we're treated to a world in which the Axis won World War II, and the United States have been divided up between Germany and Japan. In a reversal of fortunes, an American-born merchant struggles to live up to the honor codes of his Japanese occupiers, deferring to their superior wisdom not far from the honky-tonk jazz slums of San Francisco, overseen, like the rest of California, by "puppet white" governments. Copies of the *I Ching* appear everywhere like Gideons' Bibles while Germany and Japan are engaged in a race to colonize the planets (with no Cold War nuclear weapons proliferation, the money's available). A man named Baynes (an undercover Jew who's infiltrated his way into the highest echelons of German power) wonders over the innate motivations of the Nazis:

They want to be the agents, not the victims, of history. They identify with God's power and believe they are godlike. That is their
basic madness. They are overcome by some archetype; their egos
have expanded psychotically so that they cannot tell where they
begin and the godhead leaves off. It is not hubris, not pride; it is the
inflation of the ego to its ultimate—confusion between him who
worships and that which is worshipped.[5]

This kind of analysis is vintage Dick—an analysis afforded us by
way of his outrageous scenarios (technological or historical). Do we
have a sympathy pain or two as we try to imagine what it might be
like to be overcome by an archetype? Do we occasionally look in the
mirror and behold an inflated ego? If not, are we morally awake or
remotely freedom loving at all?

When Baynes makes contact with a Mr. Tagomi, in concert with
whom he hopes to reveal a Nazi military operation in the interest of
preventing global conflict, he is presented with a gift "most authentic of dying old U.S. culture, a rare retained artifact carrying flavor of
bygone halcyon day."[6] Sitting on a pad of black velvet, it's a 1938
Mickey Mouse watch (one of only ten surviving). Mr. Tagomi will
later risk his career by speaking frankly to a German diplomat of the
wisdom he's learned from the diary of a "Massachusetts' ancient
divine" whose insights appear increasingly relevant in these ego-
inflating days: "Therapeutic possibility nil. . . . In language of Goodman C. Mather, if properly recalled: Repent!"[7]

To top it all off, there is growing unrest in the occupied lands following the appearance of a book (banned in German territories)
called *The Grasshopper Lies Heavy*. Written by a certain Hawthorne
Abendsen, it conjectures a world in which the Axis lost the War and
the structure of society came out very differently. Alternately dismissed as outlandish and ridiculous and read by any and everyone
whenever they can find a private moment, it seems to be sparking a
revolution in thought. The Nazis suspect Abendsen's probably a Jew.

When characters contemplate American artifacts and say things
like, "Don't you feel it? . . . The historicity?" and reply, "What is
'historicity'?" we can note that we're neck-deep in philosophical
investigations.[8] "A weird time in which we are alive," Baynes thinks
to himself.[9] As we've already noted, Dick believed a failed appreci-

ation for weirdness or the ways in which total reality eludes us will lead to totalitarian, inauthentic human behavior. Just before Tagomi issues his call to repentance, he experiences a sort of satori concerning the biblical understanding of knowledge that haunted many an American mind:

> Saint Paul's incisive word choice . . . seen through glass darkly not a metaphor, but astute reference to optical distortion. We really do see astigmatically, in fundamental sense: our space and our time creations of our own psyche, and when these momentarily falter— like acute disturbance of middle ear . . . all sense of balance gone.[10]

Uniquely fit for the health of democracy, the elaborate thought experiments of science fiction can woo us toward a recognition of our incompleteness of vision. As we strive to pay attention to the world, we need constant reminding that just because we *feel* something (imminent threats or anger) doesn't mean it's there. Our minds, as all ancient wisdom testifies, play tricks on us. We have terrific trouble ackowledging facts that won't fit our scripts, our paradigms, or our self-congratulatory mythologies. As an American voice that won't let us hold off the biblical word on these matters as merely metaphor or primarily a "faith issue," Dick amuses us into higher awareness.

Mad America

Like Klaatu, *Star Trek*'s United Federation of the Planets, and (perhaps most powerfully) the monolith of *2001: A Space Odyssey* (1968), Ursula K. Le Guin's Ekumen gives us one possible means for imagining beyond the rhetoric that fills our minds concerning necessity, duty, goodness, and glory. Ideally, our reading of the Bible should also perform this function, but all too often we read the words and assume they're affirming all that we hold as good, true, and glorious instead of letting the Word exorcise our elaborately conceived delusions. If we take seriously the possibility of a larger frame of reference than the sovereignty of nations (a given within the biblical worldview of world without end where God alone is sovereign), we might be able to examine our language and our well-laid plans with an enhanced vigilance. When we're made to listen to our own words or look at our lives more closely, we're better able to think redemptively about ourselves.

In *The Left Hand of Darkness* (1969), Genly Ai brings good tidings to the planet Gethen on behalf of the Alliance of the Ekumen (Eighty-three habitable planets, three thousand nations), but he has to engage Gethen one nation at a time, and as we might guess, the health of all other nations, as a unity, isn't necessarily a top priority for the people "in power." And worse, King Argaven, of the nation of Karhide, in his own eyes the perfect patriot, believes that he *is* Karhide. Patriotism as selfless love of one's homeland makes sense to Genly Ai, but he comes to understand that Argaven, tragically incapable of questioning his own patriotism, will always mistake his own sense of power for love of country. And the patriotism with which Argaven congratulates himself is, in practice, more like the fidgeting fear of a cornered animal.

Needless to say, communicating with King Argaven is a difficult task. The fact that Genly Ai isn't trying to challenge him, but merely communicate, is an incommunicable fact. He offers space-travel and cosmic community to the king and his people, but Argaven can only think in terms of his own power. He only speaks the language of career ambition and survival strategy, and he's genuinely befuddled over why anyone with power would ever want to share their resources. When he asks why the Ekumen wants an alliance ("this kingdom out in nowhere, this Ekumen"), Genly Ai responds: "Material profit. Increase of knowledge. The augmentation of the complexity and intensity of the field of intelligent life. The enrichment of harmony and the greater glory of God. Curiosity. Adventure. Delight."[11] But these phrases have absolutely no appeal to the king and his sense of conservative self-possession.

As if wrestling with an insight increasingly difficult to suppress, King Agraven wonders how the Ekumen would define the word "traitor," and after sending his question via interstellar transmission, he receives an answer that only maddens him further: "To King Argaven of Karhide on Gethen, greetings. I do not know what makes a man a traitor. No man considers himself a traitor: this makes it hard to find out."[12]

When we bring this logic to bear on words like "evildoer" and "terrorist" as well as the less generously applied terms like "good man," "friend of freedom," and "great American," we see that science fiction is tackling some rather enormous issues. King Agraven angrily dismisses the Ekumen's wisdom as the kind of thing he could have procured from his own religious crackpots. But this is only the beginning of Genly Ai's ministry to Gethen and only one of Le Guin's Ekumen novels. Bringing good news to busy minds (like ours, often unyieldingly culturally captivated) will ever prove a complicated, costly business.

In *Slaughter-House Five*, Vonnegut recounts a conversation with Harrison Starr in which he reluctantly conceded that *Slaughter-House Five* was probably "an anti-war book." To this, Starr hauled out his all-purpose response to the prospect of anti-war books: "Why don't you write an anti-*glacier* book instead?"[13] And if we're looking for an anecdote to characterize science fiction's tragicomic preoccupations, I believe this one will do nicely. It's not a completely cynical take on social criticism, but it does offer an amused perspective on the question of its effectiveness.

Yet effectiveness, narrowly defined, does not always have in mind the realpolitik of the Lord's Prayer, that great cosmic equalizer of all our talk of markets, necessity, and justice. Absolute effectiveness, like unassailable security and total information awareness, is one of those mythologies no less mythical for its ability to bring up poll numbers and sell units. But the Lord's Prayer invokes that which is beyond our control, unflattering to our pridefulness, but salvific in its appeal to determined mercy and compassion as an eternal imperative for mere mortals. Vonnegut once remarked that while Einstein's theory of relativity might one day put Earth on the intergalactic map, it will always run a distant second to the Lord's Prayer, whose harnessing of energies in their proper, life-giving direction surpasses even the discovery of fire. The universe-altering phrase he has in mind is "Forgive us our trespasses as we forgive those who trespass against us." There are no zero-sum relationships in the cosmos. There is no future without forgiveness. World without end. Amen.

Chapter 6

I'm Ready for My Close-Up: Fine-Tuned Realities

We are what we pretend to be, so we must be careful about what we pretend to be.
                              —*Kurt Vonnegut,* Mother Night

They worship death here. They don't worship money, they worship death.
                              —*William Faulkner on Hollywood*

Truth is too multifaceted to be contained in a five-line summary. If the work is good, what you say about it is usually irrelevant.
                              —*Stanley Kubrick*

I didn't want you to enjoy the film. I wanted you to look very closely at your own soul.
                              —*Sam Peckinpah*

*M*y impassioned discussions with friends about what makes movies good or bad will often turn into a conversation about what we mean by "good" and whether or not something can be good without being truthful. If we recall Dylan's play with the phrase "*fictitious* story" and the Reverend Cherrycoke's authorial authority, we'll remember that truthfulness and goodness are lifetime studies in looking and listening harder, and a historically mindful consideration of the true and the good (what we sometimes mean when we say "traditional") understands that we won't always know it when we see it. In fact, a communal awareness of the "Crucify him!" impulse (if that's part of our traditional confession) carries with it a vigilance against our own hostility toward the truthful word. And our preference for tidied-up realities might be the broad path that leads to destruction in our refusal to see God's greater order for our little defensive kingdoms. When watching a movie, listening to a song, or reading the Bible, our minds shouldn't click into place too easily or too often. When they do, we might do well to wonder whether we're seeing life the way we'd like it to be or the way it is. It could be the difference between well-manufactured fantasy and moral revelation.

I hasten to add that there is probably a place for both, and I'll try to describe the difference with a story of a viewing experience. There is a moving scene in *Patch Adams* (1998) in which Robin Williams's Hunter "Patch" Adams, a medical practitioner, has painstakingly arranged a dream come true for an elderly woman whose confinement to hospitals has, in recent years, obstructed her pursuit of happiness. She has long dreamt of swimming in a pool of noodles, "Patch" discovers, and as I sat in the dark theatre watching the slow-motion sequence in which she finally has her fantasy fulfilled, I turned to my wife with tears in my eyes and said, "I hate this movie."

Please understand, I didn't begrudge the woman her moment or wish that the tale (based on a true story) had never been told, but there was something in the sequencing that felt a little like an insult, a way of cuing sentiment, and a pressing of certain heart buttons that had me feeling a little tricked. When Peter Coyote's Bill Davis, a notoriously recalcitrant patient, watches his family leave the room with the understanding that he wants to die alone in the company of "Patch" ("You're killing me, Patch," he says through pained laughter), something might strike the viewer a little amiss. I'm not saying it didn't work, because it did. The carefully programmed eliciting of my emotions, we might say, had me at Hello. But there shouldn't be a problem with wanting something a little less automatic and maybe a little more unsettling in its truthfulness.

Often accused of misanthropy for his desentimentalized way of telling stories, Stanley Kubrick once surprised an interviewer by expressing unqualified affection for Frank Capra (*It's A Wonderful*

Life and *You Can't Take It With You*). As Kubrick saw it, storytellers aren't confronted with an either/or in which they have to decide for or against emotion, but truthfulness probably requires a broader consideration than whether or not an audience will be immediately gratified emotionally: "The question becomes, are you giving them something to make them a little happier, or are you putting in something that is inherently true to the material? Are people behaving the way we really behave, or are they behaving the way we would like them to behave?"[1] This standard has a wider application than the entertainment industry. When we read the Bible or the newspaper, are we looking for an easy affirmation of our preconceived notions about life and how to live it, or are we looking for the truth of all matters? What do we mean by "objectionable subject matter"? Would that include an examination of our own lives and the consequences of our own behavior? Who among us isn't, to some degree, objectionable? Kubrick understood that the hopeful realism of unfiltered honesty is a more comprehensive stance than optimism or cynicism: "You don't have to make Frank Capra movies to like people."[2]

As aspiring learners of the good and the true, we can desire challenging stories that will edify and unsettle, illuminate and entertain, and not necessarily give up what we might call the stupider pleasures of cheap sentimentality. But if we're uninterested in anything other than eye candy, we might do well to rethink our media consumption and our understanding of goodness. Madeleine L'Engle once helpfully observed that artistic expression is only worthy of the description "Christian" if it's good. And if it is good and therefore truthful, it is, to the believing mind, Christian, unless we believe there's some fragment of truth or beauty (some secular molecule) that doesn't belong to the Lord. But again, goodness (like freedom and truth) is something we're learning about. And if Jesus of Nazareth refused to be called a good rabbi ("Only God is good"), perhaps we should watch our language with more care. We won't learn goodness and truthfulness overnight, but the Lord who began this work is perfecting it. Our education and rehabilitation are underway. We get to be people who are less concerned with whether or not they're offended, and more concerned with reorienting their sight to behold the good news of truthful storytelling.

What's in Mount Zion?

As a challenge, a comfort, a remembrance, and a possible facilitator of worship, David Lynch's *The Straight Story* (1999) holds a unique status in the history of American film. Based on a true story and adapted by Mary Sweeney and John Roach, it follows the determined, long-distance love of Alvin Straight (a representative of what Tom Brokaw calls the Greatest Generation) and his bold and costly decision to focus on the family. It is a testament to a particular, radically moral character type within American culture that has often escaped notice.

It opens with the sound of myriad insects chirping to the view of a starry sky, inviting the viewer to contemplate a universe hypnotically open, infinitely mysterious (think Hubble telescope images), and bearing a beauty we've hardly begun to fathom. We're then given an aerial view of an Iowa cornfield, drawn down to the particulars of a small town's layout, and made privy to the disorder breaking out in the life of a community as it's discovered that seventy-three-year-old Alvin Straight (played by Richard Farnsworth) has fallen down on his kitchen floor. His daughter Rosie, declared mentally incompetent by the state, expresses her distress in halting phrases. There is humor (Neighbor Dorothy: "What's the number for 911?"), but in typical Lynchian fashion, there is no judgment in the camera's observation of eccentricities. We're made to think again concerning all the seemingly discordant elements that make up our every day.

At the doctor's office, Alvin refuses to go in until Rosie (Sissy Spacek) reminds him that he promised to cooperate, and his considered, long-practiced contempt for the sterile, obtrusive complexity of health care will not allow the hip replacement his doctor recommends. Listening to a thunderstorm later that evening, he sits and contemplates his brush with mortality (he can no longer walk without the assistance of two canes), as he overhears his daughter's side of a telephone conversation and realizes that his brother, Lyle, has had a stroke. "They both been so stubborn," she says. And we begin to realize that the larger disorder haunting Alvin is his relationship with his brother. They haven't spoken to each other in over a decade.

"I've gotta go see Lyle," he announces. But the goal is complicated by Alvin's eyesight (he hasn't had a driver's license in years) and their lack of funds (Rosie sells birdhouses for a living). After a few hours of soul-searching, Alvin decides to drive to his brother's home in Mt. Zion, Wisconsin, on an ancient riding lawnmower. Toward the end of a late-night, backyard conversation in which Rosie realizes he won't be talked out of it, he says, "Look up at the sky, Rosie," as if the universe bears wordless witness to an order he can only ignore at the risk of his own soul.

"Alvin! What are you settin' out to do here?" his friends ask, scandalized by the sight of him processing, with his getup, out of the small town and onto the road. Lynch will take us across the land inch by inch, making us see the beauty we've sacrificed in exchange for our accelerated, no-time-for-it lifestyles. There are many stops and starts, including the need of a slightly less antiquated lawnmower (Alvin calmly shoots the old one with his rifle once it's failed him), and Alvin will subsist on processed meats and cheap cigars. One of the most moving scenes occurs in his interaction with a young female runaway with whom he shares his fire and his food. When she can't talk about her family he discerns that she's with child ("My family hates me. They'll really hate me when they find out"). Alvin conjectures that they probably wouldn't be so mad that they'd want to lose her or her child. She says she's not so sure about that.

Alvin recounts Rosie's loss of her own children to the custody of the state and remarks, "There isn't a day goes by that she don't pine for them kids." And then he shares a story: "When my kids were real little, I used to play a game with 'em. I'd give each one of 'em a stick and—one for each one of 'em—Then I'd say, 'You break that.' Course they could real easy. Then I'd say, 'Tie them sticks in a bundle and try to break that.' Of course, they couldn't. Then I'd say, 'That bundle—that's family.'" They talk a little more before retiring ("Lookin' at the stars helps me think"), and Alvin awakens to find the girl gone and a bound bundle of sticks beside the fire.

The film might be viewed as a slow-motion affirmation and celebration of enduring American moral values, but Lynch has been quick to point out that these long-term decisions for humanity are present in communities around the world. And the historical continuum along which they're located (lest we need reminding) is not the property of any one human-group. Alvin's witness is shared in some way with everyone he encounters, and like a Tiresias or a redeemed American Lear, his presence is an invitation to rethink our private pursuits of happiness to accommodate the hopes of the old man on the lawn-mower ("I wanna thank you for your kindness to a stranger"). The desire of the people he meets to be a positive presence within his story is intensified by his explanations. "What's in Mount Zion, Alvin?" one woman asks.

"My brother lives there," he responds. And this exchange could be a chorus to a song from *Goodbye, Babylon*. While they worry for him ("There's a lot of weird people everywhere now") and advise him to forgo the lawnmower in exchange for an easier ride, he politely asserts, "I wanna finish this one my own way." And we know that his intuitive suspicion of easily acquired reconciliation, a high-speed moral shortcut, is right on the money.

After a harrowing account of a "friendly fire" incident with a fellow veteran of World War II , he offers a bit of neighborly counsel to a pair of angry twins: "My brother and I said some unforgivable things the last time we met, but I'm tryin' to put that behind me, and this trip is a hard swallow of my pride. I just hope I'm not too late. A brother's a brother." As he nears his destination, a minister asks about the source of trouble that led to the stalemate. "Story as old as the Bible," Alvin explains. "Cain and Abel—anger, vanity. . . . Whatever it was that made me and Lyle so mad—It don't matter anymore. I wanna make peace. I wanna sit with him, look up at the stars . . . like we used to do . . . so long ago."

"Amen to that," the minister affirms. The tenderness and power of the scene in which Alvin reaches Lyle (a brief but Oscar-worthy performance by Harry Dean Stanton) is worthy of reverent meditation. And for moral edification, entertaining admonition, and wholesome storytelling (telling in the direction of the *whole*), it's not easy to imagine how Lynch could improve upon this earthy, American vision.

Recognizing Insanity

The Straight Story is a testimony to redeemed determination. Swallowing the pride that God opposes and making way for the grace that only comes to the humble, the very uppityness that turns brothers into cannibals can be harnessed for redemption's sake. But our unrepentant, manic obsessions make victims of everyone within range, and as the demoniacs of the New Testament demonstrate, they don't respond well to identification ("What do I have to do with you, Son of Man?"). Until they're recognized and talked about (painted, portrayed, put in song), their power is unchecked, dictated by its own mad logic, and veiled in an air of surface propriety. It is here that we might need to remind ourselves that truthfulness is its own gospel. If a story is really true, we need not ask, "Where was the gospel?" The good news is that truth was spoken. Truth is its own reward. Acknowledging a difficult truth (from the Psalms to Hawthorne to deathbed confessions) *is* gospel. Kubrick again: "A recognition of insanity doesn't imply celebration of it; nor a sense of despair and futility about the possibility of curing it."[3]

In Kubrick's *Doctor Strangelove: How I Learned to Stop Worrying and Love the Bomb* (1964), Peter Sellers's Captain Mandrake has to order the shooting of a Coca-Cola machine to procure the coins required to telephone a warning of a preemptive strike on Russia to a White House that won't accept collect calls. And President Muffley (also played by Peter Sellers) tries to prevent a fistfight between George C. Scott's General Buck and the Russian ambassador (Peter Bull) by crying out, "Please gentlemen, you can't fight here; this is the War Room!" Calling attention to contradictions and the ways in which our words are often an assault on meaning is the work of everyday truthfulness. Without a culture of truthfulness, there can be no democracy. And in the act of storytelling, as Kubrick observed, "The only morality is not to be dishonest."[4]

Unfortunately, our commitment to truthfulness is often co-opted by our concern over who benefits from which truthfulness. This is an understandable concern, but a radical commitment to what's true will have broader interests than who's made to look good and who looks bad when truth is spoken. If we only think in these terms, our imaginations are hopelessly sealed off from the truth that would name our idolatries. And here again, we might think of the biblical witness. Do we only apply it to the extent that it makes us look good (or our enemies look bad)? If we do, are we lovers of wisdom at all?

Do we only want gospel that says *we're* gospel in all that we say and do?

On the release of *Doctor Strangelove*, one newspaper proclaimed, "MOSCOW COULD NOT BUY MORE HARM TO AMERICA." But this is a distraction from the vocation of a culture alert to its own contradictions, eager to be spoken to, as the Proverb says, in its ridiculous folly. The truth that makes us free won't necessarily accommodate our armchair offendedness or do well in a box office that only thrives on the stories that can advertise themselves as "feel-good." Who can deliver us from our inner Mickey Mouse?

Wicked Dream

Many believe that Billy Wilder's *Sunset Boulevard* (1950) is the authoritative word on the madness that haunts Hollywood and all who fall under its spell, near and far, imitating its methods and succumbing to its cycle of mimetic rivalry (what Kubrick called an "undercurrent of low-level malevolence"). "The whole place seemed to have been stricken with a kind of creeping paralysis, out of beat with the rest of the world, crumbling apart in slow motion," remarks William Holden's Joe Gillis as he describes the home of aging silent film star Norma Desmond (played to moving and chilling effect by real-life silent film star Gloria Swanson). David Lynch once observed that it's one of those films he could watch with pleasure every day.

"Great stars have great pride," intones mad Norma in her calmer moments. But "Say you don't hate me!" is the shriek that escapes her as attentive intimacy begins to elude her again. And even when she's back in the company of Cecil B. DeMille, she can't stop herself from proclaiming, "You don't know what it means to know that you want me." Joe Gillis's slow recognition that her fan letters are forged by her butler as a peace offensive, that her friends "aren't friends in the usual sense of the word," and that Hollywood doesn't want her anymore is described as a "sad, embarrassing revelation." Watching the film fifty years on, it's hard not to notice a Norma Desmond epidemic making its way through the tuned-in Westernized world.

As we're shown a silent clip from Norma's early career, a subtitle reads, "Cast out this wicked dream which has seized my heart." And an insight concerning the ever-increasing relevance of the film begins to emerge. To what extent might visual media (Gap advertisements, magazine covers, celebrity fascination) make Norma Desmonds of us all? DeMille mentions, regretfully, that Desmond was once "a lovely little girl of seventeen with more courage and wit and heart than ever came together in one youngster" and wonders aloud over how the entertainment industry "can do terrible things to the human spirit." Neither DeMille nor Wilder would have any idea what high network ratings could be accomplished through profiling, exposing, and hiring damaged celebrities to fight and/or live together in close proximity for the cameras. The carnival barker knows how to multitask.

With Norma threatening suicide and begging Gillis to leave, he replies, "Not until you promise to act like a sensible human being." As he watches her go to any length to make herself appear more youthful while her spirit wastes away under the torment of impossible hopes and expectations, Gillis tries to speak against her delusion: "There's nothing tragic about being fifty; not unless you're trying to be twenty-five." But the wicked vision won't let go.

As a vision of the vision, *Sunset Boulevard* invites discussion about psychological disorder as a cultural export. The fascination with what celebrity status does to people's mental health (from Marilyn Monroe to Michael Jackson) is its own cottage industry. But less consideration is given to the toll taken on the viewer or, in Joe Gillis's amazing phrase, "those wonderful people out there in the dark." Shortly after *The Straight Story*, Lynch offered what I take to be an elaboration of the moral vision of *Sunset Boulevard* in *Mulholland Drive*. And if Wilder wants to suggest that the entertainment industry has a way of destroying a life every now and then, Lynch's work seems to imply an absolute annihilation of all things recognizably human. In one of the saddest, most disturbing viewing experiences I can recall (despite the momentary appearance of Billy Ray Cyrus), a story of lost identity slowly unfolds into a metaphor for dreams ("Now I'm in this dream place") turned slow-motion suicide ("Someone is in trouble. Something bad is happening"). Our female protagonists (played by Naomi Watts and Laura Harring) find themselves in possession of money and silver-screen possibilities but at the cost of absolutely everything else. The jumps in narrative logic communicate a psychic fragmentation as we begin to sense the show business payoff of a living death. "This is the girl"—a phrase spoken by directors, producers, and homicides—becomes the most chilling sentence in the film. A terror is unmasked in unconsoling fashion. The Hollywood dream place where we can check in any old time, but we can never leave. The fully commodified soul is indeed a wicked dream. It gets hold. And the nightmare undercurrent of the showing business is a power we have yet to name fully. It reaches our highest offices and our deepest dreams. Viewer discretion is advised.

A more easily viewed vision of mass-media-generated pathos is Martin Scorcese's *King of Comedy* (1983). Paul Zimmerman's story of amateur comedian Rupert Pupkin (an uncharacteristic role for Robert De Niro) features a life lived in a basement with cardboard cutouts of late-night talk-show host Jerry Langford (Jerry Lewis) and his lively guests. He fantasizes scenes in which he assures Langford, "I know, Jerry, that you are as human as the rest of us if not more so," and Langford tells Pupkin how talented he is: "You've got it. . . . How do I know? Because I envy you." All the while, his mother calls him from upstairs, asking him what he's doing, and he yells back, "I'm busy!" And in a deeply disturbing fashion, he is. In time, he'll form a kind of fan club with Sandra Bernhard's Masha (who will engage a bound Jerry Langford in the kind of conversation she'll continue in real life with David Letterman), and certain dreams, for better or worse, will come true.

It's completely ridiculous on so many levels, but, like *Sunset Boulevard* and *Mulholland Drive*, it stands up well in a world in which commodification of all things human seems to know no bounds. When Pupkin imagines being a guest on Jerry's show with his high school principal appearing to apologize on behalf of everyone who ever doubted him (thanking him now for all the joy he brings to the world), we might be forgiven for wondering if the entertainment economy instigates, facilitates, and preys on a wide variety of emotional disorders.

If covetousness and competition inevitably drive the American economy and if campaigns for public office increasingly depend on very well-funded gangs of hypnotists, it might seem inevitable that the closed dream systems they foist upon us will eventually possess our hearts, minds, and nervous systems. But there are films that demystify, inspire, and speak against the wicked dreams that have us plastering our preconceived notions over other people's faces while weighing humans out to see how they might fit within our fantasies. Alvin Straight knows that neither life nor death matter more than being reconciled, and the weak mantras of pride and personal security won't lure him away from trying to be his brother's keeper.

Our preference for imitation of life over the real thing did not begin with the advent of electronic media, but some media might suit our phantasm consciousness with particular intensity. In 2 Peter 2:3, the early church is warned against the machinery of covetousness that makes people into merchandise, the false witness that makes us think falsely of ourselves and others. Against the screenplays that reduce us to means toward someone else's end, there are testimonies that might invigorate prophetic consciousness (or, if you like, democratic consciousness). All media probably aspire toward consciousness adjustment of some sort. That's what makes a medium a medium. But learning to recognize redemptive visions amid media blitz will take some doing. As another Rupert Pupkin or Norma Desmond is probably born every minute, spreading the good news of real remembrance and real redemption will often feel like an uphill climb. But there's a kingdom coming. The fields are ripe. Redemption is under way. The film is on.

Life Can Be Beautiful

Considering all the spin with which presidential administrations, political parties, and multinational corporations seek to fine-tune reality to suit their advertisement campaigns, the filmmaker will have an interesting time distinguishing his or her work of storytelling from the image-driven ruckus vying for the attention of the masses. And it can be difficult for us, as viewers, to see past our ego-projections and our ambivalence concerning how we look and how we're succeeding compared to the confident-looking people on the screen and be genuinely engaged by a story. In the American movies that can best guarantee maximum profits (and therefore get made), the notion of self-fulfillment is often given priority over the communal ties that bind, and our tendency to externalize all evil, while viewing ourselves as well-meaning, good, and tragically misunderstood, is intensified. Ultra-violence follows.

But the rarer films that show us ourselves in all our silliness, ineptness, cruelty, and glory still survive. And learning to affirm truthfulness (flattering and unflattering) is a longer conversation than "thumbs up" or "thumbs down." We might begin by saying such things as "I don't like what that movie says." And of course, thinking and talking through what something or someone is *saying* requires a conversation. This is a good thing.

Toward the end of Clint Eastwood's *Mystic River* (2003), I apologized to my wife for making her sit through it. She accepted my apology, and we walked out of the theater in a rather depressed state. But as we discussed the story on the way home, we were less angry about all that had happened and more inclined to consider what could have happened. The more we talked, the more appreciative we became with what all parties involved had done with the story and how effectively the film (a tragedy, after all) had gotten us thinking about justice, mercy, and forgiveness.

Grateful for the unsettledness the film conjured, I was also personally taken aback by how easily we might have moved on to another subject and put down *Mystic River*, for the rest of our days, as a "depressing film." I normally pride myself on not speaking too soon, but my knee-jerk need for a place to put my feelings had almost ripped me off. Knowing my own tendencies, I'd likely have even judged people for not agreeing with me in my assessment of the film. But here we were, minds changed. Fifteen minutes older and maybe a little wiser. This too is a good thing.

In a recent reviewing of *The Wizard of Oz* (1939), I found myself eye-rubbingly taken aback by various tidbits of sentiment that now strike me as wonderfully sympathetic. If the likes of Lynch, Woody Allen, and John Sayles are crafting together and working out of a culture of common sympathy fit for democracy, we might also note the man behind the curtain who eventually tires of disguising his non-Godlikeness by admitting that he's a very bad wizard though not entirely irredeemable as a human being. And most of all, we should look hard at the last words of that horrible evildoer who wanted to do all kinds of cruel and unusual things to Dorothy, her friends, and that dog of hers. As she melts, the Wicked Witch of the West is not unaware of how strangely her well-laid plans have gone awry, and the filmmakers allow her a word of amazement concerning how her sense of justice was too simple-mindedly pursued: "What a world! What a world!" There's something rather beautiful in that.

We won't unfailingly consume media for the purpose of being humbled by the tragedy, comedy, and paradox of real life, but if we're to evade the throes of groupthink, mob fury, and other wicked dreams, we need to cultivate and sustain a taste for media that will challenge us. If we're constantly angered and defensive against anything that challenges our view of the world thus far, we would do well to wonder if we're growing increasingly hardened to the Word of God and any means by which divine gracefulness might sneak its way into our always-in-danger-of-being-hardened hearts. Fortunately, it appears that redemption not only won't give up, it's only just begun. And we don't know the half of it. We get to pay even more attention. Even better, the kingdom's coming doesn't depend upon our attentiveness. It's coming anyway. What a world.

Chapter 7

The Long Loneliness:
Experimenting with the Unexpected

I must create another system or I will be enslaved by another man's.

—*William Blake*

One who understands the nature of tragedy can never take sides.

—*Will Campbell*

The only poetic tradition is the voice out of the burning bush. The rest is trash and will be consumed.

—*Allen Ginsberg*

Let us not disdain, then, but pity. And wherever we recognize the image of God, let us reverence it, though it hung from the gallows.

—*Herman Melville*

Publick Occurrences Both Foreign and Domestick was the name of the first American newspaper. It was published by Richard Pierce and Benjamin Harris of Boston in 1690, and because they hadn't applied for the required government license, they were shut down after one issue. But the professed reason for starting the paper is worth preserving as an early freedom-loving impulse in American history and a worthwhile motivation for unsanctioned expression in any culture: "To cure the spirit of Lying much among us."[1]

Needless to say, one man's truthfulness is another man's impropriety, and a moment's consideration of the history of truth telling and

135

whistle-blowing might lead us to conclude that the termination of Pierce and Harris's operation involved more than a question of proper paperwork. But determined, committed truth seeking with life and limb requires an openness to the inconvenient truths that could drive us to shoot our televisions or sell some possessions and give money to the poor. We have to put aside the question of who's made to look good or bad by the truthful utterance if we're ever to be made free by it. This is a difficult work for human beings, but there is no apprehension of the kingdom of God or any good news for democracy without it.

There's a moment in the book of Jeremiah that describes King Jehoiakim in his palace, listening to the words of the prophet read aloud off a scroll (36:20–26). The text denounces the king's power of pride and insists that his leadership is not pleasing to the Lord ("Yet neither the king, nor any of his servants who heard all these words, was alarmed, nor did they tear their garments" [Jer. 36:24]). And Jehoiakim responds by cutting off portions of the scroll as they're read and burning them in the fireplace and ordering the arrest of Jeremiah and his secretary Baruch.

Commenting on this story, Northrop Frye once observed that the king's palace would, as Jeremiah had announced, disappear in no time while "the Book of Jeremiah, entrusted to the most fragile and combustible material produced in the ancient world, remains in reasonably good shape."[2] This is an important word, in my view, concerning the prophetic witness of God's order spoken to all our well-advertised lesser orders. Jehoiakim was king of Judah (God's chosen, we might say) and could easily lay claim to a "God bless Judah" while outlining a doomed foreign policy and ordering the arrest of the prophets. Who appears to have been put in charge, after all? But then there's little beleaguered Jeremiah, Baruch, and their pamphleteering ministry-revolution. Aren't they just asking for trouble? Why, they can write up whatever they want without anybody's say-so. Exile that Reverend Cherrycoke! Arrest Lisa Simpson and shut down that blasted Red Dress Press! Somebody oughtta *do* something.

When we say, "The Word of the Lord endures forever," are we thinking of the likes of Jeremiah and Daniel and Paul scribbling away under the shadow of a not-always-receptive empire? My own fear is that we're often in danger of thinking something more along the lines of "my understanding of reality endures forever" or "my kind of people are going to heaven." In our praise of the strong-headed, endlessly self-justifying personalities who think they're elected to project calm and buttress national confidence at all costs, we would do well to contemplate the spirit of lying, the atmosphere that makes it seem perpetually necessary for survival, and the sort of posture that is required in the successful administration of a cure.

Good Alone Is Good without a Name

Submitted for your approval, this chapter offers some brief sketches of some of America's infectious optimists. And in the spirit of Jeremiah, they all remind us, in one way or another, that the righteousness of God stands in contrast to all nations and their histories. In our temptation to view God as the blessed, profound, sacred center of what we say and do, these figures assert, often unself-consciously, that we don't know the half of it. Reinhold Niebuhr, for instance, believed that history is moving toward the realization of God's kingdom, but he also insisted that God's judgment (God's larger standard) is above and upon each new realization. Or to put it another way, we must not congratulate ourselves prematurely when there's so much further to go. We have yet to learn fully the ways of the Lord. As Abraham Lincoln suspected, we have hardly begun, if we've begun at all, to say Yes to God's purposes. An unsought awareness of our unprogress will sometimes be a jarring experience, but real, long-distance optimism requires it.

For these figures there is no theoretical Christianity, no religiosity that minds its own business, and no ideas except in actuality. No unincarnate word or disembodied faith. They're people who won't let us get away with our tendency to misconstrue the Scriptures in such a way that they no longer witness against our lifestyles (while being more than happy to use the Scriptures to speak critically of everyone except ourselves). Because they are people on whom nothing is lost, they're wary of being softened up for someone else's death-dealing program, and they all hold to the creed, through word and deed, of each and every person as "a soul of infinite metaphysical value," a phrase drawn from the theopolitical imagination of Martin Luther King Jr.

When Allen Ginsberg cries, "Slaves of Plastic!" or the Student Nonviolent Coordinating Committee (SNCC) of 1960 asserts that "nonviolence, as it grows from the Judeo-Christian tradition, seeks a social order of justice permeated by love,"[3] we might begin to envision an arsenal of mostly unused imagery and inspiration in the resistance of humanity against the nonhuman. These are a few voices of communal credibility, and I suspect they'll occupy some role in any ecumenical history of the future that considers the significance of American culture in the experience of the holy catholic church. Being a living mystery, as Cardinal Suhard says, is more effective than engaging in propaganda or rabble rousing, and these people fit the bill. And as I try to believe that all persons are living mysteries whether they realize it or not, I find the prohuman culture described here an invigorating injection for believing this way. These individuals are only too aware of the deafening propaganda of the principalities and powers of the present darkness, but they refuse to let it drown out the Word of God in a world they insist belongs to God. In the face of all the evidence to the contrary, they believe that the kingdoms of the world are being and somehow will be redeemed by the kingdom of God (Rev. 11:15). They're convinced that it is the vocation of all of God's people to start acting like it in word and deed and attitude. This is what we call apocalyptic witness, and it isn't always televised. But in the time between the times, we can look upon them with at least as much attentiveness as we're prone to accord Al Franken or Bill O'Reilly.

New Masses

As a young woman who experienced various changes in fortunes through the San Francisco earthquake of 1906 and her father's ups and downs as a newspaper journalist, Dorothy Day's preoccupation with the downtrodden was further enhanced by her reading of Upton Sinclair's *The Jungle*. After dropping out of college, she found work with New York's socialist paper *The Call* and interviewed everyone from butlers to labor activists to Leon Trotsky.

Jailed in 1917 for her role in a suffragist protest in Washington, she undertook a hunger protest and was surprised to find herself reading the Bible for comfort and encouragement. After being released with other women by way of a presidential order, her late evenings with the likes of Eugene O'Neill in a Greenwich Village saloon nicknamed "The Hell Hole" would end in the back pew of St. Joseph's Church. She'd long viewed the Catholic Church as "the church of the immigrants, the church of the poor,"[4] but her fascination with Christianity was something many of her peers found incomprehensible at best and distressing at worst.

A relationship with another journalist led to a pregnancy ending in an abortion, and she wrote about the tragedy in a novel called *The Eleventh Virgin* (which she later called "a very bad book"). With the proceeds, she bought a house on Staten Island and entered into a common-law marriage with Forster Batterham, an Englishman. With Batterham, she shared a love of nature, but her interest in Catholicism did not resonate with him. When she became pregnant again in 1925, he did not share her interpretation of the news as a miraculous turn-of-events any more than he approved her decision to have the child baptized into the Catholic Church.

"I knew that I was not going to have her foundering through many years as I had done, doubting and hesitating, undisciplined and amoral,"[5] she later wrote. And after a year, her insistence upon joining the Church herself would finalize a break with Batterham. It wasn't something she described as a great awakening, but rather a decision she felt she had to make in the direction of life for her child, her own health, and her moral vocation. During the years that followed, she would work for the Anti-Imperialist League and continue to write, supporting herself and her daughter while hoping that clarity would come.

In 1932, Peter Maurin, a French immigrant, would enter her life, and out of their conversations, the Catholic Worker movement was born. He termed the purpose of conversations and the discussions that would spread around the world out of their interaction "clarification of thought."[6] And he envisioned houses of hospitality founded for the purpose of equipping and caring for the downtrodden. In the era of the Great Depression, he felt that Christians should be less concerned with what government and religious authorities are doing and more occupied with how they might embody new creation, new ways of being human, in the glorious meantime. Beginning with the two of them, the Worker movement would consist of whoever showed up.

They began with the *Catholic Worker* paper (sold then and now for one cent), and when homeless people would show up at Day's apartment asking for the location of one of the houses of hospitality described in its pages, Day would tell them to rent an apartment and get started. In time, the Catholic Worker movement had its own building and was already well underway. An alternative community that wasn't waiting on funding or government license. It could be undertaken anywhere, and it was. By 1936, there were 33 Catholic Worker houses across the country.

"We believe in an economy based on human needs, rather than on the profit motive,"[7] Day would state on behalf of the movement, and wherever there was social upheaval (reaching out to Hispanic migrant workers in California, participating in sit-down strikes in Detroit), she would show up to say that there were Catholics somewhere on their side and that Christianity, in case someone somewhere needed reminding, did not belong solely to the rich, the powerful, or whatever political party might most shamelessly quote Scripture out of context. The paper went out and the communities formed in the interest of "the rights of the worthy and the unworthy poor" and as a witness that wherever two or more are gathered "we can work for the oasis, the little cell of joy and peace in a harried world."[8] The shared life of even a few is a witness of kingdom come and an enlistment of the mostly untapped dynamite of the gospel. We start small if we start at all.

To the oft-used question of "Did not Jesus say that the poor would always be with us?" Day had a quick reply: "Yes, but we are not content that there should be so many of them. The class structure is of our making and by our consent, not God's, and we must do what we can to change it. We are urging revolutionary change."[9]

This wasn't the only time Day drew from America's founding documents to articulate her points. The Catholic Worker movement would often have a word to say on the government's abuse of power, and a five-hundred-page file of the Federal Bureau of Investigation concluded that Day was being used by Communist groups, describing her as "a very erratic and irresponsible person." But run-ins with government and church authorities simply afforded more opportunities for clarification of thought. And at the other end of debilitating praise, she didn't like language that suggested imitation of Christ as something that wasn't the business of all Christians: "Don't call me a saint. I don't want to be dismissed that easily."[10] Doing what one can is radical enough, and what we *can* do is always more than we're accustomed to imagining. She often pointed out that anyone at all can hand out sandwiches and soap, and in this sense, the gospel waits on nothing.

According to Day, "The mystery of the poor is this—that they are Jesus, and what you do for them you do to Him."[11] But she wouldn't sentimentalize the difficulties of trying to love well. On the issue of her own shifting moods, she'd quote St. Teresa: "The devil sends me so offensive a bad spirit of temper that at times I think I could eat people up."[12] And salvation as a process (saved, being saved, will be saved) is a daily occurrence: "It is by little and by little that we are saved."[13] The long haul of neighbor love, of being good news to the poor and to the enemy, is best undertaken where two or more are gathered. Gospel happens.

Creative Trouble

I'm not sure that we could call it a thought experiment exactly, but in 1942, Bayard Rustin, a young Quaker from West Chester, Pennsylvania, who'd toured with Leadbelly, decided to try something unexpected.[14] Boarding a bus in Louisville bound for Nashville, Rustin sat in the second seat from the front of the bus. When the driver noticed and told him to sit in the back, he responded with the potentially world-altering question "Why?"

"Because that's the law," he said, "Niggers ride in the back."

"My friend, I believe that is an unjust law. If I were to sit in back I would be condoning injustice." Perturbed, but unsure how to respond, the driver repeated the routine at each stop. In time, Rustin realized the driver had made a phone call when he heard sirens and saw a police car and two motorcycles. Four policemen got on board, conversed briefly with the driver and then approached Bayard's seat. "Get up, you ——— nigger!" one of them said.

"Why?"

"Get up, you black ——!"

"I believe that I have a right to sit here, he said softly. "If I sit in the back of the bus I am depriving that child"—he gestured to a nearby child of five or six years—"of the knowledge that there is injustice here, which I believe it is his right to know. It is my sincere conviction that the power of love in the world is the greatest power existing. If you have a greater power, my friend, you may move me." As he wouldn't move they started beating him and after being knocked to the floor, he was dragged out of the bus where the beating and kicking continued. Reminding himself that resistance would lead to more kicks, he forced himself to be still. Once they slowed down, he stood up and with his arms spread out said, "There is no need to beat me. I am not resisting you."

At the sight of this, three Southern white men became agitated, got off the bus and loudly objected to Rustin's treatment. One smaller man grabbed a policeman's club and said, "Don't you do that!" When another policeman moved to strike the smaller man, Bayard stepped beween them and, facing his advocate, said, "Thank you, but there is no need to do that. I do not wish to fight. I am protected well."

An older fellow asked where they were taking him and, upon hearing that he was Nashville bound, said, "Don't worry, son. I'll be there to see that you get justice."

In the car, Rustin sat between two policemen with two seated in the front. As they shouted at him, trying to get him to lash out, he took out a piece of paper to calm himself and began to write out a passage from the New Testament from memory. "What're you writing?" a policeman beside him asked, taking the paper, reading it, crumpling it up, and pushing it in his face.

At this point, Rustin caught the eye of a younger officer in the front before he looked quickly away. Describing this moment, Rustin wrote, "I took renewed courage from the realization that he could not meet my eye because he was aware of the injustice being done." After a moment he leaned forward, touched his shoulder, and asked, "My friend, how do you spell 'difference'?"

Upon arriving at the police station, he was pushed down the hallway to the captain's office where they searched his bag and examined his copies of *Christian Century* and *Fellowship*. Eventually the captain summoned him to the desk: "Come here, nigger."

"What can I do for you?" Rustin asked.

"Nigger, you're supposed to be scared when you come here!" the captain shouted.

"I am fortified by truth, justice, and Christ. There's no need for me to fear."

The captain looked at his officers and said, "I believe the nigger's crazy!"

As he then waited at the courthouse, he heard a voice ("Say, you colored fellow, hey!"), and realized it was the older man from the bus. "I'm here to see that you get justice," he explained.

Brought before then-assistant district attorney Ben West, the policemen were asked for their side of the story and did so with much embellishment. When Rustin was asked if he would offer his account, he replied, "Gladly. And I want *you*," looking at the younger officer, "to follow what I say and stop me if I deviate from the truth in the least." Holding his eyes the whole time he'd stop and say, "Is that right?" "Isn't that what happened?" "Did I tell the truth just as it happened?" And West eventually asked him to step outside.

After an hour in a dark room, West came in and very graciously said, "You may go, *Mister* Rustin."

Rustin would later note that the possibility of the truth being heard, of the other passengers leaping to his defense, the older man's advocacy, and the young officer's unwillingness to be entirely complicit in deception, was generated by the moment he said, "There is no need to beat me. I offer you no resistance." In 1947, he would help plan the first "freedom ride" in the South in what was known as the Journey of Reconciliation and be sentenced to work on a chain gang in North Carolina.

"I believe in social dislocation and creative trouble,"[15] Rustin once remarked. And it is believed that his conversations with Martin Luther King Jr. were essential in the development of King's theopolitical strategy (Rustin would later serve as Deputy Director and chief organizer of the March on Washington in 1963). Harnessing the domination impulse (what King famously called "the drum major instinct"), redirecting it in the direction of goodness and the loving purpose that characterizes God's kingdom, can make the old world a new world. By way of improvisation, it cracks a moment open toward newer, better possibilities.

As the leading theoretician of nonviolence within the civil rights movement, James Lawson would look in the eye of a young man who'd just spit in his face and ask for a handkerchief. As the man handed him one before he could think of anything else to do, Lawson thanked him and initiated a conversation on the subject of the young man's motorcycle. Within seconds, they were discussing horsepower.

In terms of socially disruptive newness, I believe that these are the kinds of stories that will put America on the map of church history. Maurin's gospel of untapped dynamite starts to look like the only game in town. A healthy disrespect for human instrumentalities that demand exclusion and a radical reverence for human beings. A multipartisan witness that refuses to discriminate on the basis of any party affiliation. Realism redefined. Imagining the *real* world.

Mr. Jesus Is in the Streets

When Will Campbell—a lone white Baptist minister carrying a walking stick, a Bible, and a guitar case—arrived at the organizational meeting of the Southern Christian Leadership Conference in 1956, some of the younger organizers refused him admittance. But then Bayard Rustin spotted him in the hallway. "Let this man in," he insisted, "We need *him*."[16] Campbell, a former chaplain of the University of Mississippi who had accompanied students passing through angry mobs in an effort to integrate Central High School in Little Rock, would later travel to Birmingham following the deaths of four Sunday school children and participate in the long walk from Montgomery to Selma.

Ordained in a small Mississippi church at the age of seventeen, Campbell found himself increasingly estranged from much of his family and the county he grew up in, but his affection for the culture too often cast in the broad net of "bigots" and "rednecks" often had him wondering over the subtle manner in which bigotry can cut both ways. Observing as much did not always go over so well, but he was quick to point out that the stumbling block of the gospel trips up his own imagination first and foremost.

The era of the Freedom Rides afforded him many lively conversations. In one such instance, he was challenged by a newspaper editor, P. D. East, to sum up the Christian faith in ten words or less. Rising to the challenge, he proposed a summation: "We're all bastards, but God loves us anyway."[17] Not long after in Lowndes County, Alabama, a special deputy named Thomas Coleman shot and killed an Episcopalian seminarian named Jonathan Daniel. While discussing the tragic news, East wondered if Campbell's theology would hold up under duress: "What you reckon your friend Mr. Jesus thinks of all this?" Campbell said he reckoned he was pretty sad.

"Was Jonathan Daniel a bastard?" he asked. And when Campbell wouldn't respond definitively, he repeated his question.

"Yes," Campbell said.

"Well," he pressed, "was that deputy, Thomas Coleman, a bastard?"

"Yes—Thomas Coleman is a bastard."

Drawing closer to Campbell and looking him in the eye, East asked, "Which one of these two bastards do you think God loves the most?"

Campbell would later describe this moment, which followed a degree from Yale Divinity and twenty years of ministry, as his conversion experience. Through tears and laughter, he saw himself as a minister of "liberal sophistication" and, in his own words, he saw unmasked before him

an attempted negation of Jesus, of human engineering, of riding the coattails of Caesar, of playing on his ballpark, by his rules and with his ball, of looking to government to make and verify and authenticate our morality, of worshiping at the shrine of enlightenment and academia, of making an idol of the Supreme Court, a theology of law and order and of denying not only the Faith I professed to hold but my history and my people—the Thomas Colemans.

Campbell looked at East and observed, "You've got to be the biggest bastard of us all. . . . Because, damned if you ain't made a Christian out of me. And I'm not sure I can stand it."

Years later, he would attend a conference of the U.S. National Student Association and lead a discussion following the viewing of a CBS documentary called *The Ku Klux Klan: An Invisible Empire.* Disturbed by the derisive laughter that followed scenes of a clumsy young Klansman nervously trying to find his way through a military formation, Campbell began the discussion that followed with a provocative word: "My name is Will Campbell. I'm a Baptist preacher. I'm a native of Mississippi. And I'm pro-Klansman because I'm pro-human being."[18]

When pandemonium followed and most participants left the room, Campbell tried to point out how the power of particular words brought people to a boiling point. He wanted to explain the lesson he'd recently learned himself, that pro-Klans*man* is not the same as pro-Klan, and being capable of making the distinction might be our only hope for civil discourse.

"Be reconciled," sums up the ministry of Will Campbell. Borrowing the language of Second Corinthians 5, he pursues his vocation on behalf of a God busily reconciling himself to sinners through Jesus, a work, in his view, not always undertaken primarily by efforts that advertise themselves as "Christian." Viewing self-perpetuating institutions as, in large part, a corruption of Jesus' purposes, Campbell has defined the church of Jesus Christ as "one cat in one ditch and one nobody of a son of a bitch trying to pull her out."[19] This is the work of reconciliation. And it is good news.

The Final Righting of Things

To my mind, something all of these figures have in common is a steadfast refusal to view the supposed opposition *as* opposition. No one gets to claim bastardlessness, in this sense, and hell begins to follow when one person (or a culture) does. We're back to Jesus' story of the Pharisee and the thank-you-Lord-that-I'm-not-like-*that* impulse. According to these American witnesses, this is the road to annihilation. Without the larger biblical confession (*our* problem, *our* child, *our* mess, *our* life together), speech about God and grace is all too often only a reference to someone's personal, private acceptance of personal, private forgiveness; God's love for *me*. Dorothy Day could speak powerfully of a "filthy, rotten, system" (the sum total, we might say, of everyone's personal, private sin), but she did not stand aloof from it. Or as Lenny Bruce would say, "I am a part of everything I indict."

Against the paganistic, them-and-us formulations of most wars on terror, we have the dazzling realism of that most controversial of American revolutionaries, Daniel Berrigan. "I don't believe that Christians are called to win anything,"[20] he once remarked. And "unwinning" is a description I imagine he'd be more than happy to have applied to his career. There is a candor in his understanding of poetry and civil disobedience that is often missed in the haze of disbelief and conflicting feelings surrounding news of what he's said and done. And I'm not sure America has a surer, more conservative voice (in the deepest sense) on the subject of original sinfulness:

> We would like to be able to say, I can judge the world without being judged. But we know it is impossible. Because disorder lies at our heart. The drama without is the drama within, at least in an exemplary way; the one is joined to the other by the undefeated possibility of evil—the human potential for self-destruction.[21]

But as a believer in resurrection, he believes that good will triumph not only over evil but over what he takes to be his own absurd, "What else can we do?" efforts to war on war. But thinking clearly about these things and overcoming our culture's tendency to blind itself is an increasingly daunting task: "There's not much to be done about Disneyland of the mind."[22]

When Berrigan reads the Scriptures, he is moved to note that "we are unready for God; we are hardly more ready for one another."[23] And scripture that doesn't in some way dislocate our imaginings of success, victory, terror, goodness, and beauty is scripture that has yet to be read properly. Scripture calls us out of Egypt and every form of enslaving culture. But when we've reduced its liberating word to our own terms, our own idolatries, we fail to apprehend its summons to freedom.

Berrigan believes that art is that which "cries reality!"[24] As a Jesuit priest, Berrigan is especially sensitive over language that offers itself as liturgy or words of religious consolation when it's actually just a presuming of God's uncritical blessing on "more of the same. More of war, more of war preparation, more of socialized death." This sensitivity is similar to Campbell's concern over a culture that speaks condescendingly of the Ku Klux Klan while, in word and deed, behaving like "a nation of Klansmen." Berrigan was present in Selma, and his later involvement in Clergy and Laity Concerned about Vietnam resulted in his temporary exile to Latin America by Francis Cardinal Spellman (one of Lenny Bruce's favorite targets). Needless to say, his sojourn south of the border did not lessen his convictions concerning biblical witness on the subjects of peace and justice. The gradual public awareness of his role as a social critic would reach its height in May 1968 when, together with his brother Phillip and some colleagues, he conducted a ceremony that involved the burning of draft files in Catonsville, Maryland.

Six months earlier, Berrigan and Howard Zinn had embarked on a mission to Hanoi to repatriate American POWs, and this ceremony was presented as another mode of public exhortation (in a continuum with the Boston Tea Party, Thoreau's imprisonment, and the abolitionist movement) that might awaken an anaesthetized society. The creative protest of noncooperation with social madness was their witness, and when it was reported that the clerk of the Catonsville Selective Service Office cried, "My God, they are burning our records!" the irony concerning paperwork and human bodies was not lost on the judge, the jury, or the public that followed the story. It would be a few years before Daniel Ellsberg's leak of the Pentagon Papers and Robert Duvall's captain in *Apocalypse Now* describing the smell of victory as the smell of napalm in the morning, but even then, the judge was quick to qualify his verdict: "I am not questioning the morality of what you did." But the law is a human institution.

Berrigan would describe the act as an assertion and a celebration of the existence of a living God. His work is a lifelong insistence that the God of Jesus must never be reduced to an abstraction in human affairs. Death will have its dominion whenever we behave as if God isn't a concrete being to whom we're actually answerable. Practical atheism becomes our unacknowledged practice, and Christianity is reduced to a strictly "spiritual" consolation. While Berrigan aggressively resists all false witness, he doesn't speak as a confidence man or someone who would claim to be sure of the rightness of all he says and does ("A lot of life is certainly beyond me. I think it's beyond all of us these days").[25]

And the work of revolution is one of ongoing vigilance against the temptation to demonize or (once again) view the opposition as opposition: "A revolution is interesting insofar as it avoids like the plague the plague it promised to heal."[26]

In 1972, Berrigan asked, "How do we help Americans get born, get going, get growing, get moving toward recovery of intention?"[27] And we can carefully note that this question isn't a matter of personal spirituality or private faith. It's a question that assumes no such dichotomies of unhealth, and it isn't a comfortable question (especially coming from the likes of Berrigan), but it is a gospel question. It's a question about the nature of Jesus' good news, a God who is not an abstraction. Are we ready for it? Are we ready for each other? Is America ready?

Chapter 8

When the Man Comes Around: Living in Light of a Glorious Appearing

Lift me up out of this illusion, Lord. Heal my perception, so that I may know only reality.
—*Bill Hicks,* Rant In E-Minor

The Bible means justice or it means nothing.
—*Arthur Miller*

The Americans may be as vigilant as they please, but they cannot be vigilant enough for the Lord, neither can they hide themselves, where he will not find and bring them out.
—*David Walker,* Appeal to the Coloured Citizens of the World

Those who live within the least worst human world of their time have a pair of obligations: to avoid believing that the least worst is the perfect, and to stay true to what is best in it.
—*Jedediah Purdy,* Being America

*C*onfession time. Like many Americans who pass time in churches, synagogues, mosques, and temples, I have sat in relative silence through thousands of sermons. During the sermons and under their influence, my thoughts have often wandered toward my ongoing worries over eternity, and my worries, from time to time, have often assumed the form of a manic obsession. What chance do I have of getting eternity right? If you're an infidel, will you know it? Can I ever believe the right things intensely enough to get infinity taken care of so I won't have to worry about it anymore? Can I get a guarantee? Might I be incredibly, tragically wrong concerning the right answers? Should anyone dare to presume, concerning *eternity*, that they're getting it right?

As a young teenager, I paid very little attention to the sermons I sat through on Sunday mornings and Sunday evenings, because I was too busy reading through the Bible. I wouldn't have said that reading the Bible would get me to heaven, but, if pressed, I might have explained that I wasn't willing to take any chances. I didn't like the thought of the Lord returning and finding me a wishy-washy servant who hadn't read the Bible all the way through, and, to be completely candid, I wasn't completely pleased to imagine the Lord returning at all. I dared to hope that such a return might be good news for me, but I didn't suspect it would be good news for most of humanity, the quick and the dead, who probably had even less of a chance of believing the right things than I did. I worried and prayed for the son of Yul Brynner's Pharaoh in Cecil B. DeMille's *The Ten Commandments*, because he had kicked Moses' staff and mocked him, not knowing the gravity of what he was doing, and he was taken by the angel of death before he could repent or be baptized. I suspected he was not alone in his unfortunate ending. I imagined millions were similarly endangered, and I wasn't sure how I should feel about it.

In those days, I believed that the thirteenth chapter of the Gospel of Mark referred to the second coming, and I was especially intrigued by verses 32–37. They seemed to say that the only thing certain about that dreadful day was that no person would be expecting it. Matthew's Gospel said it would come like a thief in the night, and to my mind, this sounded like the one guarantee concerning a coming day with no reassuring guarantees and not much in the way of good news for most people. So in the thick of my obsessing over eternity, I devised a plan.

What if we organized an around-the-clock Keep Awake vigil? If the Scriptures promised that the Lord wouldn't come back when anyone was expecting it, why not make sure we had someone at all times sustaining a personal sense of expectation? The burden could be shared in shifts just so long as each person understood and felt committed to their responsibilities. For the duration of a half-hour time slot, anyone who felt so inclined could sign up to take a turn imagining that the

Lord might be coming back at that very moment. We could keep the vigil going until everyone everywhere had had plenty of time to start believing the right things about the Lord. We'd have more time to get ready. *I'd* have more time to get ready. For the love of humankind and the eternal fate of most people, it seemed like a good idea. And because I believed that loving other people was most obviously what the Lord required of us, I even entertained the hope that the plan might please him. Maybe I wasn't the only one to notice this very helpful loophole. Maybe it had been put there to be lifted out by a clever, dutiful reader like myself.

I don't share this testimony as a joke or to denigrate anyone's eschatology. But I imagine there is something familiar here, for many Americans, in the suspicion that God's ultimate purposes will involve a vast ethnic cleansing to end all ethnic cleansings. Needless to say, I don't share this suspicion, but I wonder about the question of empathy in the minds of citizens (not always limited to those who consider themselves "religious") who feel sanctioned to view other people as target markets, hell fodder, collateral damage, infidels, or irredeemable non-souls. Do we fancy ourselves somehow godlike when we deem our opponents (liberal, conservative, anti-American) beneath our contempt? Do we think we're doing the Lord's work when we steal a campaign sign from someone's yard or e-mail a cartoon that makes the person we'd never vote for look stupid? Do we assume God will "take care of" all the people who'll never understand how good we are? Do we hope God will happily dispose of all those unreasonable people who hate our freedoms?

The biblical witness, in my view, is a countertestimony to all our antihuman reductions as it calls us to pray for, love, and radically seek the welfare of anyone we've come to view as the enemy. And God's faithfulness to all generations will always surpass whatever we think we know about people and what they deserve. It is the vocation of the church to uphold the human as the bearer of the divine image against the drumbeat of nationalism, market devaluing of the human, and every form of mob hysteria. But as we've seen, the witness will often be subordinated as a side issue, a misplaced sensitivity, or an insane dissent that will only aid the evildoers. Or else, the witness will be held off as irrelevant to the political sphere and reduced to that nebulous, harmless, vapid realm the market calls spirituality. How are we to go about properly valuing ourselves or others within these categories? What will be the content of our values talk? How might we hope to get control of our vain imaginings, wicked counsel, and lying tongues?

The Trouble with Groupthink

On this side of the coming kingdom, it could be that the closest a twenty-first-century world power will ever come to formally recognizing an instance of possession by a deluding spirit is the report, to which we've already alluded, in which the Senate Intelligence Committee invoked "groupthink" in an effort to describe the faulty decision-making process whereby government employees seemed incapable of correctly observing the evidence before their very eyes. On the issue of weapons of mass destruction in Iraq, we'd been told that the absence of evidence is not the evidence of absence and that we mustn't distinguish between Saddam Hussein and the Al Qaeda network in our talk of war on terror, but here was the use of Orwellian language to describe what had gone wrong, a name to describe the unseen forces that battle it out in the formation of public opinion. Did this make Karl Rove and Dick Morris our groupthink gurus? Do campaign operatives traffic in anything less than groupthink manipulation? What are the methods of an advertising campaign anyway? Are their methods unsound?

A culture of groupthink will cultivate its own institutional belief structure (principality, power, team spirit) and our ability to think and see clearly will often fall victim to its persuasiveness. Neither Rod Serling nor the apostle Paul stands alone in their warnings of atmospheres in which honest questions provoke outrage and testimony that fails to fall in sync with the herd is viewed with angry suspicion. But who benefits most from the careful manipulation and maintenance of these atmospheres? What becomes of the general welfare? Who watches the watchers?

I'm not calling for a Department of Exorcism, but I do occasionally entertain a hope for an American culture rigorously committed to resisting the pleasures of groupthink. When I speak of pleasures that require our vigorous resistance, I don't mean to knock the sense of belonging for which Gloria Desmond, Rupert Pupkin, Alvin Straight, and all of God's creatures naturally pine. But there is an intoxication available to us in the form of blissed-out lockstep, a strength in numbers, and a kind of pseudocommunity united by escalating aggression toward whatever person or people-group it might momentarily brand the source of all unease. Groupthink works as a uniter, because we want to feel safe and strong more than we want to be wise, and we often habituate ourselves to a laziness of thought that has us drifting toward whatever power can most aggressively ridicule all opposition while extending a word of "Come unto me" to the confused masses. The siren song of groupthink sells.

The New Testament provides numerous words of admonition and careful articulations of this elusive, multiheaded appeal to our self-preserving instincts, and the most provocative of them all is antichrist. The term is so often abused that we're often loath to use it, but we might do well to utilize the term when we're in the presence of mythic realities gone murderous, when hatefulness, buttressed by myth, begins to spread like a contagion, and when we're prone to mistake immoderate intensity of passions for strength of character. When we're willing to name antichrist thusly, we might discover that our mental furniture is better equipped to resist the magnetic pull of groupthink. Experience shows that groupthink works because it feels good. Groupthink sells units and wins votes, but it can't make the world safer for democracy. It doesn't like authorial authority, Romney Wordsworth, or that pesky notion that no insignificant person has ever been born. We're all especially susceptible to antichrist when our sense of self-preservation outweighs the call to love and enjoy our neighbors, but we're deaf to the possibility of confession when we only see antichrist in other people claiming peace and justice and deliverance from evil.

Disenthralling ourselves from the elaborate mythologies of other people's power struggles is a tall order, but it's a crucial work if we're to avoid becoming an America that can't stand to be questioned, Americans more in love with their preferred mythic reality than the lives of people who have yet to fit within their side of the mythic Them and Us. To the extent that we're uncurious, uninterested in the differences between Iraq and Iran, and unmoved by any testimony that doesn't confirm our advance publicity, we're caught in the throes of what Orwell called doublethink, the mind trick whereby citizens learn to deny freedom to their own minds. As we buy into the projections of strength, calm, and victory we demand of our elected leaders, we become tragically closed to the biblical witness against our pridefulness, and the gospel is no longer a living element within our vain imaginations.

As Karl Barth and his fellow Evangelical Christians understood in their response to the Reich Church Administration in 1934, the confessions of the Jewish Christian tradition are a challenge to every form of groupthink, especially when those who claim an affiliation with God begin to rally hearts and minds under a nationalistic banner. When this occurs, it is the prophetic consciousness that brings a redemptive skepticism to our mythic realities. The confessing community can speak candidly and demand candor when career politicians and celebrity pundits feel trapped by a public that seems to only want promises of absolute victory in the war on evil, further proclamations of America's moral superiority, and assurances concerning the innate goodness of the American people. The confessing community is called to disrupt the feedback loop of self-congratulation, to speak back to the Us and Them sales pitch, and to bear witness to the scandalously multipartisan posture of God's war on terror made known in the life and ministry of Jesus of Nazareth.

Karl Barth understood that Jesus' gospel is represented falsely whenever it's viewed as a truth among other truths, a novel opinion among others, a whispering chaplain to human instrumentalities, or a private faith option with nothing to say to anyone's national pride or spending habits. It isn't a position, but a cosmic reality. And Barth believed that God's kingdom sets a question mark up against all our mythic realities, principalities, and rabble-rousing words. This kingdom undermines all our death-dealing idolatries. It belongs to no nation, and it will allow no other allegiances to stand alongside it. Its scope is without end, and it is under way. It makes all things new. It is stronger than death.

Failures of Imagination

When the 9/11 Commission Report famously cites a failure of imagination as a central issue facing the United States in its response to the possibility of terrorist attacks, we're probably prone to most immediately think in terms of the difficulty of imagining all possible threats and all the numerous stratagems by which hostile forces seek to threaten our health and property. And a script for the future that features seekers and holders of public office devising new ways to assure voters that they, and they alone, are capable of imagining every imaginable threat to America's perceived self-interest is not a promising prospect for public discourse. But there are larger moral possibilities in an acknowledgment of a deficient national imagination, and as I hope I've at least begun to demonstrate in this book, American culture contains a greater arsenal of imaginative witness than we're liable to remember as we speak in conversation-stoppers, thrown back and forth by a politics of what-aboutery, too often speaking as if we're threatening somone, building up to a backhand slap. The more unimaginative we become in our responses to conflict, the more we play into the screenplay of terror, more fully becoming the caricature America's self-professed enemies describe.

But the American moral imagination, at its redemptive best, can be a power that enables others to think and see differently. George Washington asserted that the Declaration of Independence was a claim, on the part of the colonies, to the rights of all of humanity, and, in an interesting paradox, he believed that the rights, for which the colonists fought, should be applied to enemy combatants. He wanted British prisoners to be treated with more humanity than the colonists received at the hands of British soldiers. When the war was over, thousands who fought against America's independence chose to remain in the land where they would enjoy more rights than they could hope for elsewhere.

Does this kind of story still have a place among the mythic realities that make up America? Or would Washington be ridiculed for thinking that the British might be impressed with our sensitive side? Are we losing the ability to understand why Washington's prisoner policy was a good move and a sound investment in the future? Might we envision some parallels as we seek to cultivate and maintain a multipartisan imagination?

In 1860, Abraham Lincoln coined what would become a Republican Party slogan when he articulated a faith-based initiative that might not play too well in our day: "Let us have faith that right makes might, and in that faith, let us, to the end, dare to do our duty as we understand it." The quotability of this particular sentence often distracts from the morally subversive quality of Lincoln's words. The pursuit of proprietary happiness, in this case slavery, has long been buttressed by the tragic consistency of *might* making right in history. History as written by the proprietary winners who can always outgun and outmaneuver the less fortunate whose fate is dictated by force of arms. But Lincoln challenges his audience to assume a more costly commitment of pursuing right against the immense pecuniary interest of the powerful who hold one-sixth of the population as slaves. There is a righteousness that transcends our perceived self-interest, and we get to pursue it in the hope that a better self-interest (not necessarily pragmatically verifiable) will follow. We get to live in hope of a better health than we're currently defending at all costs, including, perhaps, the forfeiture of our souls.

And as ever, the Through-a-Glass-Darkly clause (dare to do our duty *as we understand it*) that marks all careful speech is witnessed in Lincoln's admonition that we can only speak, see, and understand fallibly. A determined awareness of our deficient imaginations will mark all talk of God, evil, freedom, and necessity (a difficult temptation in an election year), but if a nation or its leaders are to resist the drive to consider godlikeness as something to be grasped, this confession must never be cast aside. The crucial quality of this redemptive qualifying of our words is something Barth and Lincoln held in common.

On the difference between a warrior community that lives by unacknowledged piracy and a compassionate people who fear their fortress impulse and seek to live the good neighbor impulse because their souls depend upon it, the farmer essayist Wendell Berry has a timely word. As Brand USA is often in danger of being viewed as a force more predatorial than redemptive in the non-American world, Berry's words sit well alongside the findings of the 9/11 Commission:

> I think the only antidote to that is imagination. You have to develop your imagination to the point that permits sympathy to happen. You have to be able to imagine lives that are not yours or the lives of your loved ones or the lives of your neighbors. You have to have at least enough imagination to understand that if you want the benefits of compassion, you must be compassionate. If you want forgiveness you must be forgiving. It's a difficult business, being human.[1]

At our redemptive best, Americans hunger for more effective ways of being positively human. We're drawn to stories and songs that help us make better sense of our own struggles, our successes and failures, and we're edified to see ourselves reflected in the infinitely valuable everyone else. We seek the sober realism that shows us we're not the only ones with a desire for freedom as we understand it and all the all too clearly human drives which, in their determination to destroy other people's evil, only serve to make matters worse. Violence begetting more violence in a tragically unimaginative downward spiral.

The imaginative neighborliness to which Washington and Lincoln alluded risks much on the hope that right is its own might, that wisdom will somehow be vindicated over brute strength, and that the judgments of the good Creator are good and righteous altogether over and against all of our attempts at Babels and Babylons and balance of power. It risks much on a redeeming God who resurrects and restores, and it dares to hope that God's revolution will one day bring good out of our destructive foolishness. To genuinely believe that a loving God esteems human life more highly and compassionately than we can understand is to embrace a more uplifting worldview than the ancient tribal impulse of Them and Us and a wider world than an endlessly adversarial culture can comprehend.

Some of These Days

Who or what do we have in mind when we try to imagine a loving God? Even if we believe that there's nothing to be done to merit the love of God, that all fall short, do we nevertheless harbor the notion that some of us are falling a little less short than others? Do we think of some nations or people-groups as pretty well irredeemable? Do we draw a line in the sand between the OK and the not-OK? Is it our way or the highway?

The Americans in the previous chapter struggle with these questions in an out-loud manner worthy of our contemplation. In one way or another, they all wrestle with the gospel of Jesus. And while they try to live in witness to it with glad, reckless abandon, believing that there's no other way to go, they're all too honest to say that the love of God is obviously a pleasant thing. It is a consolation, but if it consoles everything we value, leaving our darker impulses unchallenged, have we really begun to give it much time? Have we really thought hard about all that it includes? All that it embraces? Do we really want to get in on this kind of thing? Do we think we're prepared for God's No Spin Zone?

I find the amused and moved conversion experience of Will Campbell very helpful in this regard. By his account, he's beginning to be confronted by a cosmic order *founded upon* the forgiveness of sins. What a horrible mess for our sense of truth and justice! What an undoing of any and all hierarchy! If we begin to believe that God *likes* our enemies, how will it impact the way we talk about them? Have we even begun to sense the ways divine generosity trumps our offendedness? I imagine his laughter and his tears, and the image of a fool-loving Maker with very specific hopes for that multiple-pilgrim species called humanity inspires the need for constant, daily revision in the way I esteem myself, my neighbors, and the people on the television screen. The gospel challenges us to turn our clichés into lived realities, to revalue devalued people, and to think harder about our own thinking, thus representing the better, coming world in our tired and troubled one.

"Some of these days" is an especially effective phrase to characterize the extreme makeover of the coming kingdom, in which the different way of doing things is more fully inaugurated (Jer. 31:31–34), a grand rejuvenation occurs (Ezek. 34:25–31), and God's righteousness occupies all of creation (Isa. 66:18–24). It envisions a future hope that colors our thinking and doing in the present. And the Lord's Prayer invites a robust living out of this new order as a prayer for the wit and invigoration to respond to abounding grace in the here and now. *Those* days aren't completely unrelated to *these* days.

If we reduce this hope to a future dispensation mostly divorced from the present or imagine that the way of life Jesus introduced isn't to be bothered with until some time after "the Rapture" (a suitable theology, incidentally, for a fully privatized faith), the possibility of earth-bound, incarnate witness is tragically vitiated. In a spirit contrary to the lives of Dorothy Day and Daniel Berrigan, a contemptuous attitude toward "the world" develops among ostensibly religious people who think their faith is primarily a matter of what happens to their spirits when they die.

But the cosmic significance of Jesus' resurrection reaches further than disputed boundaries in the Middle East and worries over the United Nations. It changes everything now. The sovereignty of the once-crucified, now-risen Lord doesn't wait for events in Jerusalem. The here and now is being sanctified already, and all authority in heaven and on Earth is the Lord's. There is a coming day, a new order, some of these days, but if we aren't especially invigorated by it now, if it doesn't inform our sociopolitical imagination now, what are we expecting then? Do we want it in the meantime? Does the love of God infect our view of other people?

Dead People Walking

In N. T. Wright's *The Resurrection of the Son of God*, Wright opens the final section ("Easter and History") with an amusing excerpt from Oscar Wilde's *Salome*. Herod has received word that there is a man who's been raising other men from the dead. Herod doesn't like this: "I do not wish him to do that. I forbid Him to do that. I allow no man to raise the dead. This man must be found and told that I forbid Him to raise the dead. Where is this man at present?"

"He is in every place, my lord," the witness explains, "but it is hard to find Him."[2]

In its portrayal of a confused ruler who's just been confronted by an elusive yet ubiquitous peasant defying the well-established rules of the game, this exchange rather brilliantly introduces the political significance of Easter. Herod is terribly displeased by all this, because resurrection is bad news for anyone whose power depends on lethal force. He doesn't want dead people coming back. That ruins the whole point of his illustrious career. It means that history isn't written only by winners, and that might might not make right. The "silenced" aren't ultimately silenced. They might come back with a word, and an especially authoritative "Once upon a time. . . ." The once-sure thing of ruling by the sword is being delegitimated. Victory over death deprives power of its primary means of persuasion. There are no closed books.

When resurrection is taken seriously, those "ethical considerations" that are often cast aside in a cynical or despairing fashion might suddenly take on more weight. "What can we do about it now?" is no longer the ultimate conversation stopper. History isn't simply the memory of states. And pondering over how many died, and why, and how necessary it was is no longer a luxury a "realist" can't afford, because reality isn't quite what we thought it was. Yet we might say that the pondering is "politically correct," but only because the polity (and that which it might deem "correct") has been redefined. It now includes the interests of dead people. What really happened takes on a disturbing new relevance.

It wasn't a compliment and his concerns were never pursued, but "Spotty Lincoln," a young Illinois congressman during the Mexican war, wanted James K. Polk to admit that the spot where blood was first shed in the conflict was not on U.S. soil. These were Abraham Lincoln's "Spot resolutions." It matters, Lincoln insisted, because *right* makes might. The living concern with what really happened (and not simply with whether or not the living can be persuaded to be pleased later on) will occasionally distinguish a culture. It's a sense of rightness that enlarges perceived self-interests. And divine judgment resides over it, calling us to larger considerations than whatever we think we might get away with. If an apocalyptically authentic No Spin Zone is really coming on earth as it is in heaven, who among us can stand?

"Elimination of potential rivals," "collateral damage," and "antipersonnel weapons" take on a different aura when resurrection is brought into play. And "worthy is the lamb who was slain," as an announcement of Jesus' kind of Lordship and the kind of honor, power, glory, and praise that characterize the cosmos, marks a politics of resurrection. Hitler once insisted that success is the only earthly judge of right and wrong. But Easter overturns whatever inhumanity might manage to proclaim itself a success, sanctifying the human form for all history. A radical humanism is born.

When Martin Luther King Jr. insists that when it comes to human beings, the image of God is never totally lost, he's operating within this continuum. Humans will require the utmost reverence from now on. They can't *not* matter. Necessity that suggests otherwise is forever delegitimized. Lenny Bruce was especially troubled by standards that claim to maintain all that's right and true while playing fast and loose with human life: "My concept? You can't do anything with anybody's body to make it dirty to me. Six people, eight people, one person—you can do only one thing to make it dirty: kill it. Hiroshima was dirty."[3]

Come on, Pilgrim

Any consideration of the significance of a resurrected Jesus requires a long look at why a world would find him distasteful. Woody Guthrie's "Jesus Christ" is a robustly orthodox song in its insistence that American culture (like all others) would not have him, and while this is probably an uncontroversial point for anyone willing to voice the traditional prayers of confession, we're often in danger of assuming, without much thought, that we're not the kind of people who would put Jesus to death. We sometimes presume we're in general agreement with what Jesus has to say, as if all "decent, God-fearing people" are. But a consideration of the personalities in the previous chapter and a casual glance at the Sermon on the Mount might have us wondering if we haven't created for ourselves a domesticated Jesus. Does American Christianity suffer opposition? If so, is it resisted for its Christ-likeness? Is there a continuum?

I believe that there is. But we're often guilty of assuming continuity with unthinking presumption, speaking of Jesus as if he is easily incorporated into our lifestyles while viewing too radical an apprenticeship to his lifestyle as unseemly or irreverent. We rightly put him on a pedestal (Jesus' perfect life), but this can sometimes serve to place real discipleship out of consideration. In this sense, I often think that people who at least take Jesus seriously as a teacher, as the wisest individual who ever lived, are entering into the kingdom in ways that those who only want to have their sins removed for the afterlife aren't. If our interest in Jesus as an atoning sacrifice cancels out our attentiveness to the things he did and said, something has gone horribly wrong. Do we want the benefit of God's blessing *minus* the specifics of Jesus' commands? Do we think there's a difference?

When we think of his lifestyle as King and Day and Berrigan force us to do, we see him as a real-world individual that human society can hardly tolerate. It was this sort of realization that W. H. Auden cited as the reason for his conversion. While Muhammad and Buddha and Confucius struck Auden as reasonable figures not too difficult to agree with, he experienced Jesus as a stumbling block, a man whose visions elicited from Auden's heart the words "Crucify him." In Auden's view, it isn't the case that, if there were no Jesus, we'd probably invent him, because Jesus' summons to a different order, a kingdom coming, subverts all our favorite, sanctified orders and mythic realities, exposing and undoing our unacknowledged groupthink.

But have we transmogrified Jesus to suit our human instrumentalities? On the question of who killed him, many Americans would agree with Mel Gibson that we all did. But do we daily acknowledge our hostility to his kingdom, noting all the ways that we do not acknowledge him? Do we recognize the crucifying impulse in our anger toward the neighbor, the opponent, or the enemy combatant? Do we try to make it a private issue?

It's important to remember that Jesus' civilization doesn't come to us naturally. If we forget, we mistake our good intentions for God's purposes and become a Babylon impenetrable to prophetic witness. If Jesus' gospel, the announcement and description of God's kingdom, is the standard by which all human orderings will be judged (our politics measured by his), how are we doing? What will it mean for America when the cosmos is liberated from its Egypt? Are we on the Lord's side in this process? Will we know how to call it good news? Do we know now? There are no foregone conclusions in these discussions, and according to the Jewish Christian tradition, all manner of things will somehow be made well. But what do we think this means? Will we know the smell of victory? Is it what we're looking for?

Yonder Come Day

In the spirit of Kurt Vonnegut and a little dash of Walker Percy's *Lost in the Cosmos*, I'd like to offer a fanciful scenario in the interest of sparking a thought. A "What if?" for the Waffle House contingent, submitted in the hope that readers might begin to make up their own. This is only a poor sketch to serve as a friendly provocation. Dig, if

you're willing, a picture, or a thought experiment. It's a day like any
other day. It's morning again in America. And word eventually comes
to you that the president is going to be on television to make a special announcement, so you tune in. The president appears with an odd
look, not nervous exactly, but somehow unwound and no longer
sporting the obligatory confidence Americans expect in a president.
And there seems to be a look of genuine surprise and perhaps an aura
of relief. The speech begins:

> My fellow Americans. I bring you good tidings. Something tremen-
> dous has come up. Something wonderful. To be frank, many of us
> have given lip service to this event over hundreds of years, but we
> were all alike in ignorance. We did not know that of which we
> spoke. It was Thomas Jefferson who once remarked, "I tremble for
> my country when I reflect that God is just." As I speak to you now,
> I am intensely aware of the inadequacy of my speech, and I am
> pleased to know, as I never dreamt I'd be, that I will not stand before
> you in this capacity again. My fellow Americans, the Lord is among
> us. He appeared at the East Jerusalem YMCA today in conversation
> with people who happened to be near at hand. And we're still unsure
> as to what this means, but we do know this: The Lord's rule goes.
> This will involve many adjustments. And while much is still unfore-
> seeable, we can be assured that it is good news. The steadfast love
> of the Lord will never cease. In our nation's history, we often swore
> our oaths with our hands pressed on a collection of documents that
> forbade oaths, and we often believed we were handing out or deny-
> ing sovereignty to nations even as we read that God alone is sover-
> eign. We raged with a sense of sovereignty, we plotted and schemed,
> and we often believed we were just. We were rebellious and we did
> not know what we were doing. But now, the way of the Lord is on.
> No good thing will go unrestored. His way of living life and giving
> and loving is the way things are and were and will be. The Lord is
> here. It is possible that we are approaching the days when none of
> our flags are still there, but the star-spangled universe was never
> dependent on them. The nations will now continue to prove the glo-
> ries of God's righteousness. Truth is marching on and making us
> free. God's mercies never come to an end. It is good. Good morn-
> ing. Blessed be the name of the Lord . . . (static)

What would something like this mean? What do we imagine would
follow the end of the transmission? When we imagine God reigning

forever and ever, do we give much thought to what that forever would look like? Does it include the kinds of things Jesus said in the Sermon on the Mount? If we think of the kingdom, as we're taught to pray, as a new order on earth as it is in heaven, what does it change about our today? What does it mean to "repent, because the kingdom of God is at hand"? It is good news, but is it what we have in mind when we say gospel? Is our gospel good news for everybody? Have we drawn lines in the sand that the Lord doesn't recognize?

I suspect we have. And I believe we do well to entertain all kinds of thought experiments when we contemplate the meaning of the prayers we pray, prayer as a determined experiment in trying to see the truth about ourselves: the tragic, the comic, the precious, the ridiculous, the out of control, and the angry. The Lord's Prayer has an amazing way of relativizing our have-to's, calming our nerves, and recontextualizing many a needful thing. The prayer invites us to reorient our hopes in the direction of resurrection and rejuvenation, reconciliation and redemption, not just for our kind of people, but for all of anxious creation, all nations, and the whole beloved, not-American world.

We Have the Right to Remain Silent

Americans are possessed by a wide variety of stories about who matters, who no longer matters, who's the most despicable liberal/conservative pain-in-the-neck, and who out there will "get what they deserve" when they're finally put down or thrown out of office, and stories whose only conceivable end is one of terror for someone else. These stories, in some form, have always been with us, but according to the gospel, they inevitably hide the reality of things. The apocalypse of the coming kingdom doesn't offer itself as one story among many or a "Wouldn't it be nice?" for the "spirituality" section of our psyche. The apocalypse resides over all matter and history.

If we believe that Jesus' good news describes the real world, our lesser stories will be subordinated. Our understanding of what's absolutely necessary (for personal happiness and homeland security) will be transformed by it. But it could be that this process is most immediately obstructed by our inability to stop talking or in any way quiet down our chattering minds. As I've already pointed out, I suspect the agreed-upon contempt for "spin" in public discourse is a beginning of a recognition of this problem, but it only goes so far when it's always someone else's spin that gets us worked up. We have to become aware of our own spin, our own unwillingness to be objective, and our own rage at a challenging word to our groupthink. We don't have to fire off an opinion about every conceivable issue at a moment's notice in the workplace, at the Waffle House, or in front of a camera. We can refuse knee-jerk defensiveness and opt for silence. And if we're going to perceive apocalypse making its way into our busy, chattering every day, we have to. We can pray and occasionally keep silence. We can watch and pray. We might begin to feel our ignorance and be sobered as we see that not only do we not know where we're going, but we don't know exactly where we are right now. We're neck-deep in mystery. When we put on the speech habits of Cherrycoke, Lincoln, and the apostle Paul, we might find ourselves inclining closer to a truthfulness toward which none are particularly disposed. We might learn to keep silence as we constantly remind ourselves of our fallible visions.

Silence might sober us long enough that we'll repent of the ways our tough talk presumes omniscience. It might deliver us from the death-grin of self-satisfied self-confidence. We might begin to see the ways the gospel intersects with the news of the day and the ways the word of the Lord will make us see and speak differently. We won't have to know all the details of salvation, redemption, and the end of history, but we will know that Jesus is never a separate issue. His story and the community he gathers around himself are political, a sacred community whose power is somehow louder than bombs. A radical remembrance belongs to these people, because they believe that Jesus' career was the definitive breakthrough of God's kingdom. Any authority that tries to reduce this community to a "spiritual" zone is speaking with a false objectivity, because the kingdom to which this community tries to bear witness encompasses reality. And repentance is the word for the speech and action that acknowledges the distance between our proud little kingdoms and God's larger order, power, and glory, which are forever. It cannot be controlled, bought off, or ultimately silenced. And within it, our delusions are being subsumed. The Lord is risen.

Notes

INSTEAD OF AN INTRODUCTION

1. Dwight D. Eisenhower, "President Dwight D. Eisenhower: Farewell Address, January 17, 1961," http://members.tripod.com/~edyl/jfk/ikefw.html.

2. Martin Luther King Jr., "Beyond Vietnam" (speech, Riverside Church, New York, April 4, 1967).

3. Gregory Wolfe, "Fugitive Energies, *Image Journal* 29 (Winter 2000), http://www.imagejournal.org/back/029/editorial.asp.

4. Thomas Pynchon, *Mason & Dixon* (New York: Henry Holt, 1997), 349.

5. John S. Mbiti, *African Religions and Philosophy,* 2nd ed. (Oxford: Heinemann, 1989), 141.

CHAPTER 1: THE ANGEL IN THE WHIRLWIND

1. N. T. Wright, *The New Testament and the People of God* (Minneapolis: Fortress Press, 1996), 350.

2. Ibid., 353.

3. Norman Mailer, "Only in America," *New York Review of Books,* March 2003, 50.

4. Arthur C. Cochrane, "Barmen Declaration," in *The Church's Confession under Hitler* (Philadelphia: Westminster Press, 1962), 237–42.

5. George W. Bush, "The President's Address to the Nation" (speech, New York, September 12, 2002), http://usinfo.state.gov/usa/s091102.htm.

6. Maya Jaggi, "Signs of the Times," *The Guardian,* October 2002.

7. All movie quotations are taken from my own transcription.

8. Stanley Hauerwas, "The Tonto Principle," *Sojourners Magazine,* January–February 2002, 30.

9. William Pfaff, "The Question of Hegemony," *Foreign Affairs,* January–February 2001.

10. Wolfe, "Fugitive Energies."

CHAPTER 2: SONG OF OURSELVES

1. Robert N. Bellah and others, *Habits of the Heart: Individualism and Commitment in American Life* (Berkeley: University of California Press, 1985), 221.

2. Ibid., 235.

3. Harold Bloom, *The American Religion: The Emergence of the Post-Christian Nation* (New York: Simon & Schuster, 1992).

4. George W. Bush, interview by Tom Brokaw, *Nightly News*, NBC, April 24, 2003.

5. Shakespeare, *Macbeth*, act 3, scene 4, lines 134–39.

6. Ibid., act 3, scene 4, lines 134–35.

7. Herman Melville, *Moby Dick*, A Norton Critical Edition, ed. Hershel Parker and Harrison Hayford (New York: Norton, 2002), 139.

8. Ibid., 143.

9. Ibid.

10. Ibid.

11. Walt Whitman, *Leaves of Grass* (New York: Signey, 1955), 41.

12. Ibid., 43.

CHAPTER 3: NO CELESTIAL RAILROADS

1. F. O. Matthiessen, *American Renaissance: Art and Expression in the Age of Emerson and Whitman* (London: Oxford University Press, 1941), xv.

2. Ibid.

3. James McIntosh, *Nathaniel Hawthorne's Tales: Authoritative Texts, Backgrounds, Criticism*, A Norton Critical Edition (New York: Norton, 1987), 55.

4. Ibid., 57.

5. Ibid.

6. Herman Melville, letter to Nathaniel Hawthorne, April 16(?), 1851, http://www.melville.org/letter2.htm.

7. Nathaniel Hawthorne, quoted in Matthiessen, *American Renaissance*, 321–22.

8. Herman Melville, *The Confidence Man: His Masquerade*, A Norton Critical Edition (New York: Norton, 1971), 158.

9. Hawthorne, quoted in Matthiessen, *American Renaissance*, 32.

10. Nathaniel Hawthorne, *The Scarlet Letter*, ed. Seymour Gross (New York: Norton, 1988), 53.

11. Ibid., 61.

12. Ibid.

13. Ibid., 76.

14. Ibid., 99.

15. Ibid., 116.

16. Ibid., 100.

17. Ibid., 175.

18. Melville, "Hawthorne and His Mosses," in *Moby Dick*, 527.

19. Melville, "Hawthorne and Mosses," 525.

20. Melville, *Moby Dick,* 103.
21. Ibid., 104.
22. Ibid.
23. Ibid.
24. Ibid., 57.
25. Ibid., 34.
26. Ibid., 36.
27. Nathaniel Hawthorne, *The House of the Seven Gables: A Romance* (Cutchogue, NY: Buccaneer Books, 1987), 201.
28. Melville, *Moby Dick,* 21.
29. Ibid.
30. Ibid., 53.
31. Ibid., 54.
32. Ibid., 56.
33. Ibid.
34. Ibid., 79.
35. Ibid., 98.
36. Ibid., 300.
37. Ibid., 74.
38. Ibid., 156.
39. Melville, *Confidence Man.*
40. Ibid., xiv.
41. Ibid., 58.
42. Ibid., 59.
43. Ibid.
44. Richard Gray, *The Life of William Faulkner: A Critical Biography* (Oxford: Blackwell, 1994), 272.
45. William Faulkner, *The Sound and the Fury,* ed. David Minter. A Norton Critical Edition (New York: Norton, 1994), 203.
46. Ibid.
47. William Faulkner, *Go Down, Moses* (New York: Vintage, 1942), 331.
48. William Faulkner, *Absalom, Absalom* (New York: Vintage, 1936), 218.
49. Ibid., 392.
50. William Faulkner, *As I Lay Dying* (New York: Vintage, 1930), 223.
51. William Faulkner, *Light in August* (New York: Modern Library, 1932), 47–48.
52. Faulkner, *As I Lay Dying,* 165.
53. Faulkner, *The Sound and the Fury,* 222.
54. Ibid., 226.
55. Ibid., 48.
56. Ibid.
57. Ibid., 78.
58. Ibid., 130.
59. Ibid., 120.

60. Ibid., 143.
61. Ibid., 181.
62. Ibid., 37–38.
63. Ibid., 183.
64. Ibid., 185.
65. Ibid.
66. Ibid.
67. Thomas Pynchon, *V* (Philadelphia: J. B. Lippincott Co., 1963), 366.
68. Thomas Pynchon, *Vineyard* (Boston: Little Brown, 1990), 195.
69. Thomas Pynchon, *Gravity's Rainbow* (New York: Viking, 1973), 167.
70. Ibid., 164.
71. Ibid., 262.
72. Ibid., 350.
73. Ibid., 571.
74. Pynchon, *Mason & Dixon,* 9.
75. Ibid.
76. Ibid., 10.
77. Ibid., 31.
78. Ibid., 7.
79. Ibid., 31.
80. Ibid., 411.
81. Ibid.
82. Ibid., 412.
83. Ibid., 252.
84. Ibid., 253.
85. Ibid.
86. Ibid., 73.
87. Ibid., 361.
88. Ibid., 395.
89. Ibid., 511.
90. Ibid., 345.
91. Ibid.
92. Ibid.
93. Ibid., 307.
94. Ibid.
95. Ibid., 346.
96. Ibid.
97. Ibid., 641.
98. Ibid., 347.
99. Ibid., 30.
100. Ibid., 350.
101. Ibid., 354.

CHAPTER 4: BLOODIER THAN BLOOD

1. Ishmael Reed, *Mumbo Jumbo* (New York: Doubleday, 1972), 11.
2. Ibid., 216.
3. Ibid., 217.
4. Ibid., 6.
5. Flannery O'Connor, *The Complete Stories* (New York: Farrar, Strauss, and Giroux, 1971), 132.
6. William Blake, "Annotations to Bacon's *Essays Morals, Economical, and Political,*" *The Complete Poetry and Prose of William Blake,* ed. David V. Erdman (New York: Anchor, 1988), 623.
7. John Gerome, "Country Legend Johnny Cash Dead at 71," *Detroit Free Press,* September 12, 2003, 142.
8. Robert Shelton, *No Direction Home: The Life and Music of Bob Dylan* (New York: Beech Tree Books, 1986), 200.
9. Ibid., 203.
10. Ibid., 211.
11. Bob Dylan, interview by Nora Ephron and Susan Edmiston, Summer 1965, http://www.interferenza.com/bcs/interw/65-aug.htm.
12. Shelton, *No Direction Home,* 260.
13. Bob Dylan, *Live 1964: Concert at Philharmonic Hall—The Bootleg Series,* vol. 6, Columbia/Legacy.
14. Tony Tanner, *City of Words: American Fiction: 1950–1970* (New York: Harper & Row, 1971), 178.
15. William Faulkner, *Requiem for a Nun* (London: Chatto, 1953), 85.

CHAPTER 5: THE SIGNPOSTS UP AHEAD

1. Philip K. Dick, "The Android and the Human," in *The Shifting Realities of Philip K. Dick: Selected Literary and Philosophical Writings,* ed. Lawrence Sutin (New York: Vintage, 1995), 187.
2. Ibid.
3. Ibid., 187–88.
4. Philip K. Dick, "My Definition of Science Fiction," in *The Shifting Realities of Philip K. Dick,* 100.
5. Philip K. Dick, *The Man in the High Castle* (New York: Vintage, 1962), 41–42.
6. Ibid., 44.
7. Ibid., 237–38.
8. Ibid., 63.
9. Ibid., 150.
10. Ibid., 233.
11. Ursula K. Le Guin, *The Left Hand of Darkness* (New York: Ace Books, 1969), 34.

12. Ibid., 39.

13. Kurt Vonnegut Jr., *Slaughterhouse-Five or the Children's Crusade: A Duty-Dance with Death* (New York: Dell, 1968), 3.

CHAPTER 6: I'M READY FOR MY CLOSE-UP

1. Tim Cahill, "The Rolling Stone Interview: Stanley Kubrick," in *Stanley Kubrick: Interviews,* ed. Gene D. Philips (Jackson: University of Mississippi Press, 2001), 198.

2. Gene Siskel, "Candidly Kubrick," in *Stanley Kubrick,* 187.

3. Eric Nordern, "Playboy Interview: Stanley Kubrick," in *Stanley Kubrick,* 68.

4. Martha Duffy and Richard Schickel, "Kubrick's Grandest Gamble," in *Stanley Kubrick,* 168.

CHAPTER 7: THE LONG LONELINESS

1. *Publick Occurrences Both Foreign and Domestick,* September 25, 1690, http://www.sims.berkeley.edu/academics/courses/is182/s01/031.gif.

2. Northrop Frye, *The Great Code: The Bible and Literature* (San Diego: Harvest, 1981), 200.

3. The Sixties Project, *Student Nonviolent Coordinating Committee Founding Statement,* http://lists.village.virginia.edu/sixties/HTML_docs/Resources/Primary/Manifestos/SNCC_founding.html.

4. Jim Forest, "A Biography of Dorothy Day," in *The Encyclopedia of American Catholic History,* ed. Michael Glazier and Thomas J. Shelley (Collegeville, MN: Liturgical Press, 1997). Also available online at http://www.catholicworker.org/dorothyday/ddbiographytext.cfm?Number=72.

5. Dorothy Day, *Selected Writings,* ed. Robert Ellsberg (Maryknoll, NY: Orbis Books, 1992), 33.

6. Ibid., xxv.

7. Forest, "A Biography of Dorothy Day."

8. Day, *Selected Writings,* 98.

9. Ibid., 111.

10. Ibid., xviii.

11. Ibid., xxxvi.

12. Dorothy Day, *House of Hospitality* (New York: Sheed & Ward, 1939). Also available at Dorothy Day Library on the Web, http://www.catholicworker.org/dorothyday/daytext.cfm?TextID=442.

13. Dorothy Day, *Selected Writings,* xiii.

14. Bayard Rustin, *Time on Two Crosses: The Collected Writings of Bayard Rustin,* ed. Devon W. Carbado and Donald Weise (San Francisco: Cleis Press, 2003), 2–5.

15. Martin Mayer, "The Lone Wolf of Civil Rights," *The Saturday Evening Post,* July 11, 1964. Also available online at http://www.reportingcivilrights.org/authors/selections.jsp?authorId=133.

16. Thomas L. Connelly, *Will Campbell and the Soul of the South* (New York: Continuum, 1982), 88.

17. Will D. Campbell, *Brother to a Dragonfly* (New York: Seabury Press, 1977), 218–23.

18. Ibid., 243–47.

19. Ibid., 187.

20. Daniel Berrigan and Lee Lockwood, *Absurd Convictions, Modest Hopes* (New York: Random House, 1972), 211.

21. Daniel Berrigan, *Consequences: Truth and . . .* (New York: Macmillan, 1967), 56.

22. "A Conversation between Daniel Berrigan and Alan Fox," http://www.rattle.com/rattle11/poetry/interview.html.

23. Daniel Berrigan, *Jeremiah: The World, The Wound of God* (Minneapolis: Fortress, 1999), xii.

24. Daniel Berrigan, *Poetry, Drama, Prose,* ed. Michael True (Maryknoll, NY: Orbis, 1988), xi.

25. "A Conversation between Daniel Berrigan and Alan Fox," http://www.rattle.com/rattle11/poetry/interview.html.

26. Berrigan, *Poetry, Drama, Prose,* 285.

27. Ibid., 267.

CHAPTER 8: WHEN THE MAN COMES AROUND

1. Wendell Berry, "Heaven in Henry County," interview by Rose Marie Berger, February 2004, http://www.sojo.net/index.cfm?action-magazine.article&issue-soj 0407&article-040710.

2. N. T. Wright, *The Resurrection of the Son of God* (Minneapolis: Fortress, 2003), 684.

3. Ronald K. L. Collins and David M. Skover, *The Trials of Lenny Bruce: The Fall and Rise of an American Idol* (Naperville, IL: Sourcebooks, 2002), 3.

9 780664 227692